The pic Wild Essex

compiled, edited
and designed by

Tony Gunton

Lopinga Books

Published by Lopinga Books
Tye Green House, Wimbish, GB-Essex, CB10 2XE

First published 2019

Text & maps © Tony Gunton 2019

Front cover painting by Alan Harris

Photographs © as credited, otherwise by Tony Gunton

All rights reserved.

Except for copying of small parts for the purposes of private study or review (as permitted under the copyright acts) no part of this publication may be reproduced, stored in a retrieval system, or transmitted in any form or by any means, electronic or otherwise, without the prior permission of the publishers and copyright owners

The right of Tony Gunton to be identified as the author of this work has been asserted by him in accordance with the Copyright, Design and Patents Act 1988

ISBN 978-1-9164631-9-6

British Library Cataloguing-in-Publication Data
A catalogue record for this book is available from the British Library

Printed by Remous Print, Sherbourne

The Nature of Essex Series No. 10

Contents

Acknowledgements	4
About this book	5
More Wild Essex apps and books	5
Geographical index	6
Key to notation used in entries and on maps	8

Places to go by habitat

Ancient woods	9
Grassland and heath	35
Forests	59
Parkland	81
Estuary and coast	99
Rivers and wetlands	129
Reservoirs and pits	147
Industrial relics	161

Indexes

Index to sites	168
Index to species photographs	170

Acknowledgements

Wildlife conservation charities

Many of the sites in this book are owned or managed by wildlife conservation charities. These charities encourage visits by non-members but depend on their members to help them acquire and manage their nature reserves, as well as campaign for wildlife conservation generally.

Essex Wildlife Trust and London Wildlife Trust are local organisations (although membership is open to anyone, wherever you live). Both are part of the national Wildlife Trusts partnership.

The National Trust, the Woodland Trust and the Royal Society for the Protection of Birds are national organisations that work in Essex and throughout the country.

All these organisations have been supportive during the preparation of this book and its previous editions. If you enjoy visiting the places in this book, please support one or more of the wildlife charities that work for wildlife in Essex by donation or by joining them as a member.

Photographers

The photographers whose colour photographs are such an important part of this book supported us by allowing us to use their work free of charge, either following a direct request or via a Creative Commons licence. Without this generous help this book would have been much the poorer.

Photographers are credited on each image (and those with no credit are my own). Some of them earn their living as wildlife photographers. Anyone wishing to contact them regarding use of their work should be able to find them on the Geograph (geograph.co.uk), Flickr (flickr.com) or wikiMedia (commons.wikimedia.org) websites.

Other important contributors

Many people have contributed to the making of this book, such as by providing information and by checking the entries for the sites under their care. We thank them all for their generous support and help.

Disclaimer

We have made our best efforts to produce a comprehensive and accurate guide but no doubt errors remain. Information that was correct in June 2019 can also, of course, go out of date. If you rely on certain facilities or are keen to see something in particular, please check the latest situation via the web or by contacting the site manager before setting off on a long journey. Wildlife is inherently unreliable and the author and publishers accept no liability for loss or inconvenience resulting from any errors or omissions in this book.

The maps are designed to give visitors a good indication of what they will find when they visit a site. They should not be taken as a definitive statement of rights of way or of boundaries.

About this book

This book follows in the footsteps of *Wild Essex*, published in 2000, and *Explore Wild Essex*, published in 2008, both of which also served as Essex Wildlife Trust's reserves handbook. Here, as in earlier versions, Essex is defined as the old vice-county of Essex, extending into Greater London as far as the River Lee in the west.

Unlike its predecessors, this book includes only a selection of the best sites in Essex. One reason for this change is that Essex Wildlife Trust now has its own reserves handbook, which it gives to new members when they join, and also there are now many other ways to find out where to go, including my own website www.wildessex.net and my own app for smartPhones, both of which cover all 300+ wildlife sites in Essex. Selecting the best sites also means that the book can be slimmer and cheaper than its predecessors.

In *Wild Essex* the 170 sites existing in 2000 were arranged in alphabetical order by name, with groups of adjacent sites included under a collective name. By 2008 the site count had grown to more than 260, so in *Explore Wild Essex* they were separated into ten regions, from Tendring in the far east to Uttlesford, Epping Forest and the once-Essex parts of London on the western fringe.

Here, they have been sectioned up by habitat, each section beginning with a description of the habitat and its key features. One advantage of this is that descriptions of individual sites can be shorter and can focus on the particulars. If you do come across an unfamiliar term in a site description, turn back to the beginning of the section and you should find it explained there.

The 120 sites included this book are in my view the *crème de la crème* of Essex, all worth a long visit and, if necessary, a long journey. As in earlier editions, details of public transport options are provided for each site. To help you find them by road, postcodes are included to feed into satNavs as well as grid references.

The maps show footpaths as they exist at the moment and, for the more complex sites, also recommended routes that will take you through all the best habitats.

Overleaf is a geographical index, in other words a map of Essex showing the positions of all the sites with page references. There is a conventional alphabetical index of sites at the end of the book.

Tony Gunton
August 2019

More Wild Essex apps and books

The *Explore Wild Essex* app is available from the iTunes and Google Play app stores. This app provides all the information included in this book and also lets you follow the paths, and your own position, on a satellite map, so you never need to get lost on a big or complex site. It also covers another 160 (at the current count) mostly smaller sites not included in this book.

Walk Wild Essex (ISBN 978-0-9530362-9-5) is a companion book describing over 50 different walks in every part of Essex and east London, many easily accessible by train or tube. Available from bookshops or visit the Wild Essex website *www.wildessex.net* to order online. An app is available also, currently only from the iTunes app store.

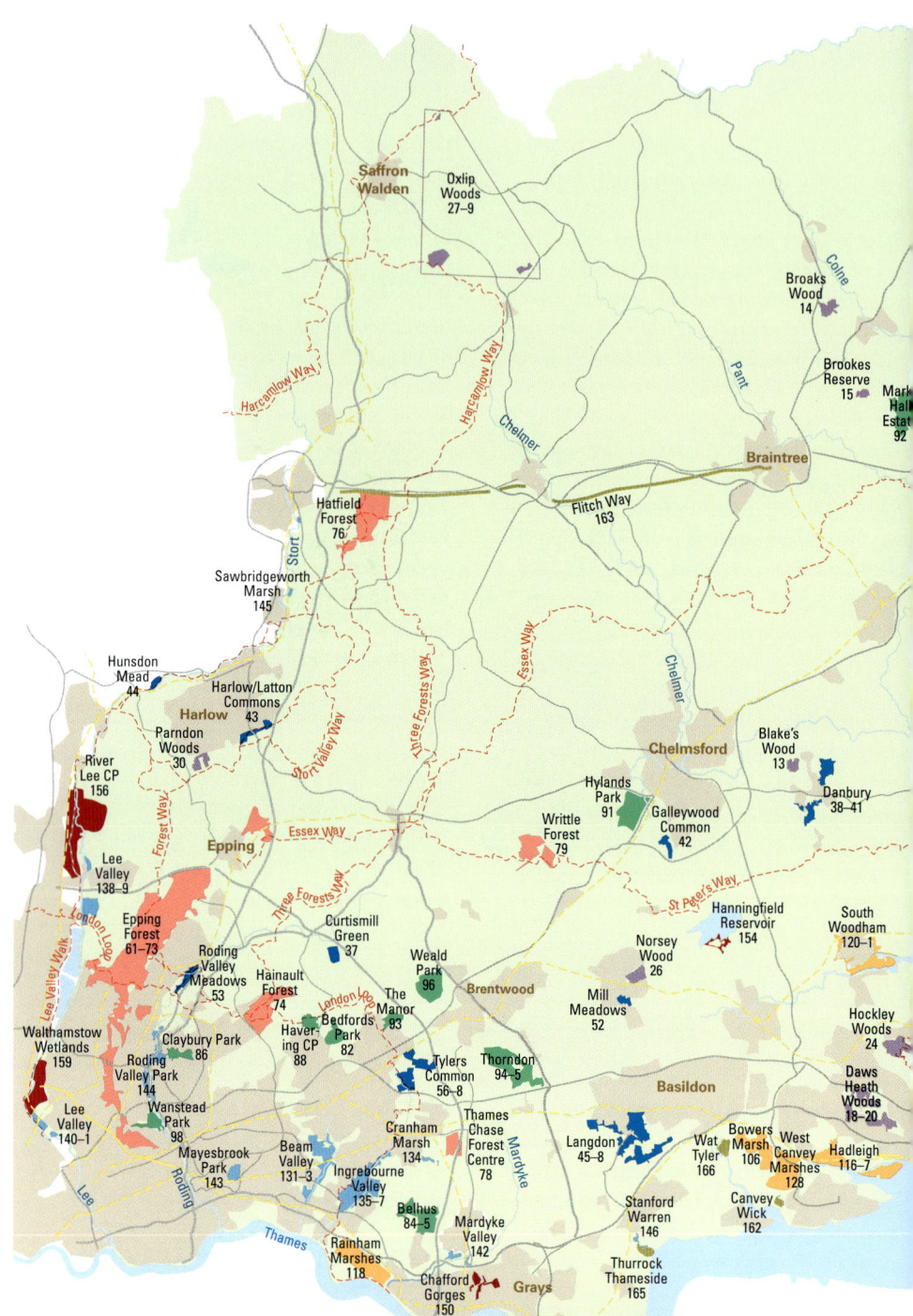

Geographical index

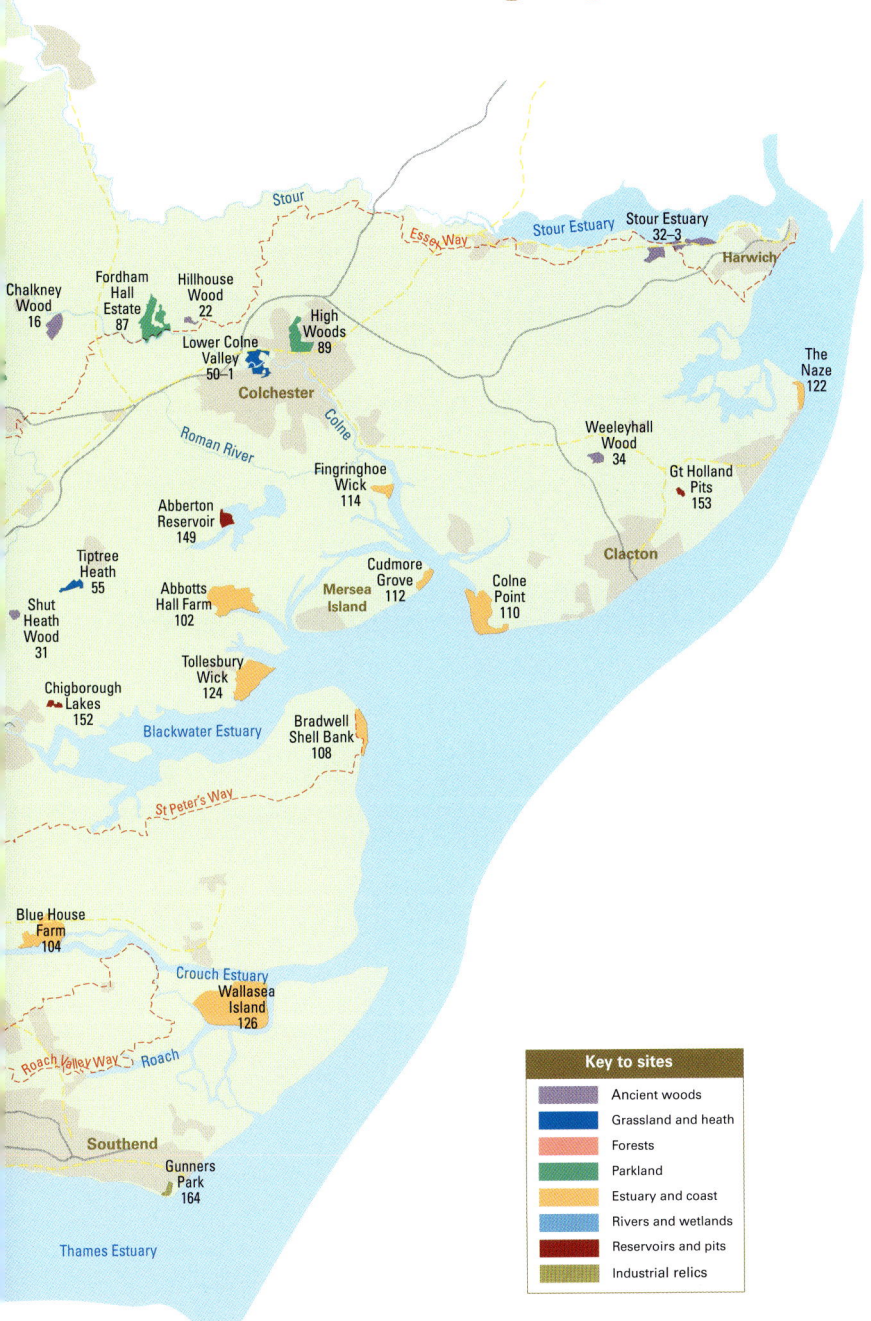

Main entries in *colour*; sub-entries in *grey*

Abbotts Hall Farm

700ac/280ha   CO5 7RZ   TL 963 146   SSSI (part), SPA

- Size in acres and hectares
- Postcode for SatNav
- OS grid reference
- Designations (see key below)
- Organisation chiefly responsible for management

- How to get there
- Public transport
- Opening times
- Best time to visit
- Facilities/notes for disabled visitors
- Facilities for bikes
- Restrictions/arrangements for dogs
- Guidance for visitors

SSSI   Site of Special Scientific Interest
Area notified by Natural England as important and with statutory protection.

SAC   Special Area of Conservation
SPA   Special Protection Area
Areas strictly protected under the European Birds and Habitats Directives.

NNR   National Nature Reserve
Nature reserve of national importance, managed by Natural England (not always with public access).

LNR   Local Nature Reserve
Nature reserve of local importance, established by a local authority (usually with public access).

Key to maps

Vegetation
- grass or heath
- amenity grass
- scrub
- woodland
- new woodland
- marsh/fen
- reed bed
- saltmarsh
- mud
- sand or shingle
- arable

Water bodies
- fresh/brackish
- salt

Site boundary

Facilities
- visitor centre
- museum
- bird hide
- play area
- picnic area
- pub
- refreshments
- parking
- " with fee
- " informal
- " disabled
- toilets

Paths
- foot only
- in between[†]
- wheelchair
- bridleway/horse ride
- recommended

Features
- sea wall
- bank or cliff
- church
- golf course
- viewpoint
- building
- built-up area

Entrances
- vehicle
- other

Roads
- surfaced
- other/track

[†] *surfaced paths suitable for people with walking difficulties and possibly usable by wheelchairs, e.g. with assistance*

Ancient woods
Shaped by generations of woodsmen

Woodsmen have been managing our woods since the Middle Ages, and very probably since well before then. Wood was used to build houses, ships, fences and many other things, and later to fuel the charcoal furnaces of the industrial revolution.

In the 20th century these markets declined, and many woodlands were either grubbed up or neglected. For wildlife, neglect was almost as bad as destruction, because without management the canopy soon closes in and woods become dark and bare and, with no cover and little food, most of the wildlife moves out.

Coppice-with-standards

The form of management practised, almost uniquely, in our lowland woods, is known as *coppice-with-standards*. This was designed to provide the woodsman with a good living year after year, but it also happened to create ideal conditions for a wide variety of wildlife. Under a coppicing regime canopy trees, usually oak, were grown at intervals of 20m or so and harvested when big enough to provide structural timbers for houses, bridges or ships. Low-growing trees were planted underneath, known as the *underwood*, and this is what provided the regular income. They would be

Ancient woods

Charcoal kiln at Pound Wood

Wood stacked after coppicing

coppiced, that is cut to ground level, on a cycle of between six and 20 years, depending on the species – hazel, used for fencing and thatching spars, on a short cycle; sweet chestnut providing rot-resistant stakes and hornbeam for charcoal, on a longer cycle.

As the woodsmen coppiced their way round the wood, they created a series of glades at different stages of regrowth – at the beginning of the cycle, sunny clearings full of wild flowers, in turn attracting pollinating insects, grading up to shady glades with ferns at the end. Over the centuries, our native wildlife adapted to this regime. Primroses, for example, can sit dormant for years, waking up and flowering when coppicing lets in the light.

Woodbanks and ditches

After coppicing the underwood trees regrow rapidly, but in the early stages they are vulnerable to animals such as deer, which stunt or kill the trees by browsing off the young shoots. To prevent this, ditches were dug around woods and the earth thrown up on one side to form a bank, on top of which a fence was constructed. This formed a formidable obstacle even for agile animals like deer.

Of course the fences are long gone, but networks of banks and ditches are a characteristic feature of large blocks of ancient woodland. Ditches were also used to mark ownership boundaries.

The decline of coppicing

Coppicing is barely viable commercially now, even with a buoyant market for firewood, but some of our remaining ancient woods are being coppiced for conservation reasons, and part of the cost recovered by selling firewood or charcoal. Forestry Commission is achieving much the same by removing the conifers that it planted in many ancient woods and allowing the original native trees to regenerate.

These are the most rewarding woods to visit, retaining the diversity of appearance and wildlife that mediæval woodsmen first brought about.

Ditch and woodbank lined with aged hornbeams

Ancient woods

Woodland butterflies

Woodland butterflies suffered badly from the decline in coppicing. Most of them relied on particular flowering plants as food for their caterpillars, such as dog violets, but as the canopy closed in and those plants were shaded out, so the butterflies disappeared. By the middle of the 20th century Essex had lost all its fritillaries and the purple emperor, and the white admiral was just hanging on.

In the 1990s the heath fritillary was reintroduced into Hadleigh Great Wood and several other coppiced woods in the south of Essex, and now it is well established. This butterfly depends on open glades within woodland where the food plant for its caterpillars, common cow-wheat, can be found.

More recently, other woodland butterflies have returned (see below). It may be that coppicing has opened the door to them and the warming climate has let them in.

Oxlip woods

Woods in the north-west corner of Essex grow on chalky soils of boulder clay, and these have unusual variety and are unusually rich in flowering plants. These are the woods where oxlips – looking like a mixture of primrose and cowslip – can be found, which grow nowhere else except the area where Essex, Suffolk and Cambridgeshire meet.

These are also the woods in which you are most likely to see deer, especially fallow, introduced from the continent by the Normans, but also the native roe and another introduced species that is no bigger than a labrador dog, the muntjac.

Heath fritillary

Oxlip

Three butterflies making a comeback in Essex woods *(from left)*: white admiral *(flies July to early August)*, silver-washed fritillary *(mid-July to end August)* and purple emperor *(early July to mid-August)*

Ancient woods

Deer are a problem in woods that are being coppiced because they browse the young regrowth and may kill the trees, so often they are fenced out of newly coppiced areas.

Woodland seasons

Ancient woods look their best in spring when flowers such as bluebells and wood anemones flower before the trees put on their leaves, often in spectacular numbers. They also sound their best in spring when nesting birds sing to establish their territories.

Birds, small mammals and many more animals do well in coppiced woods because the dense understorey that develops provides food and cover for nesting. Much of the animal life of woodland is secretive and the trees make the birds difficult to see even when you can hear them. So if you want to make the most of woods in spring you need to learn birdsong and take binoculars with you.

In summer, woodland clearings and rides can be full of life on sunny days, with bumblebees and other pollinating insects taking advantage of the sheltered conditions, and maybe a hawker dragonfly cruising around picking a few off for lunch.

Visit in autumn for late flowers, for fungi and for changing leaf colours.

Alan Williams

Fallow deer

The most prized edible fungus: the Cep or Penny Bun

…and the deadliest: Death Cap

Ancient woods

Blake's Wood

104ac/42ha   **CM3 4AU**   **TL 775 064**   **SSSI**

Blake's Wood is famous for its spring flowers, with sheets of wood anemones giving way to spectacular displays of bluebells, while in summer its more open areas are full of foxgloves. Other flowering plants include yellow archangel, early purple orchid, twayblade, moschatel and wood spurge.

The trees are mainly hornbeam and sweet chestnut coppice, with oak, ash and birch standards, and it has well defined ancient banks and ditches.

Breeding birds include warblers, nightingale, woodpeckers and treecreeper. Purple hairstreak butterflies can be seen around the oak trees in high summer. In autumn the wood is rich in fungi.

In Danbury to the north of Riffham's Chase, Little Baddow. From the A414 approach via The Ridge, a mile north of Eve's Corner, or via Riffham's Lane further west.

Bus services Chelmsford to Maldon and Chelmsford to S. Woodham Ferrers. Get off at Riffham's Lane.

Accessible at all times.

April to June for wild flowers and songbirds; October for fungi.

Twayblade *flowers June–mid-July*
Adrian Knowles

Roger Jones

Broaks Wood

155ac/62ha   CO9 1UP   TL 784 317

Forestry Commission

This is a large working woodland with an average of 500 tonnes of timber harvested annually, but conservation is given a high priority. Where introduced timber trees are harvested, for example, the original native broadleaved trees are replanted or allowed to regenerate naturally. The traditional method of coppicing is used also, on species such as sweet chestnut, hazel and ash.

As a result the wood is rich in wildlife, including familar plants such as bluebells and primroses, and also some rarities. For example, it has a scattering of wild service trees and, in the stream valley to the east, opposite-leaved golden saxifrage. Also, there is a grove of giant redwoods.

It has several ponds and some damp areas filled with sedges. There is a good chance of seeing fallow deer, and it is a good place to see bats, feeding in the glades and along the rides at dusk.

Glyn Baker

Main entrance on Hedingham Road (A1017 Braintree–Hedingham) between Gosfield and Sible Hedingham.

Bus service Braintree to Castle Hedingham runs along Hedingham Road.

Accessible at all times.

Spring for woodland flowers and birdsong; summer for flying insects.

Opposite-leaved golden saxifage
flowers mid-March–May

Ancient woods

Brookes Reserve

59ac/24ha **CM77 8BA** **TL 808 268** *SSSI (part)*

This wood is named after Thomas Brookes, the 18th-century owner. It comprises 40 acres of ancient woodland and some 18 acres of former arable fields that have been planted up with native trees. It is coppiced on rotation to produce charcoal and firewood.

Most of the wood is ash and hazel coppice, with areas of small-leaved lime and hornbeam and more than 20 wild service trees. Thirteen ponds and the wet surface are evidence of the chalky boulder clay soil.

Bramble, pendulous sedge and dog's mercury dominate the ground flora, with large areas of primrose, but it also has some unusual plants, including greater butterfly orchid, twayblade and herb paris.

Nuthatch and treecreeper nest here, along with many summer migrant songbirds. Brown hares and herds of fallow deer can often be seen.

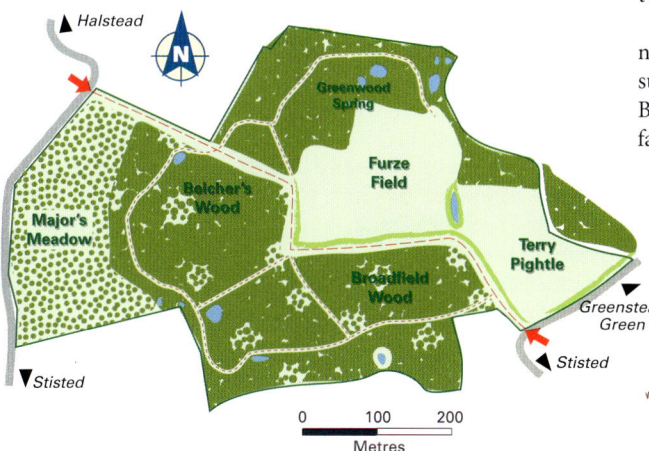

Herb paris *flowers mid-May–June*

Between Stisted and Greenstead Green north-east of Braintree: from Greenstead Green the reserve is about 2km down on the right and from Stisted 3km down on the left just past Tumbler's Green. Park with care on the verge.

Hourly bus service Halstead–Braintree.

Accessible at all times. The car park is locked except by arrangement to prevent misuse.

For songbirds, a sunny morning in April/May; a warm summer afternoon for butterflies; early October for autumn colours.

 Please keep dogs on a lead.

Ancient woods

Chalkney Wood

200ac/80ha   *CO6 2LD*   *TL 872 273*   *SSSI*

Chalkney Wood is unusual in its great variety and also contains the greatest concentration of small-leaved lime trees in Essex. Small-leaved lime is the dominant species in much of the southern part of the wood, which is on a boulder clay soil. This gives way to London clay as the land falls towards the River Colne in the north, and as it falls so the natural vegetation contains more and more hornbeam.

The south-western part is owned and managed by Essex County Council. The remainder, running down to the River Colne, is owned by Forestry Commission who planted up much of it with conifers. As these conifers are harvested, the original native trees are being allowed to grow through and take their place.

Probably because of a patch of particularly chalky soil, the southern corner contains a mix of ash, hazel, holly, field maple and wild cherry, with wild currant growing beneath them. Along the north-western edge are a number of alder valleys fed by springs, where marsh marigold, opposite-leaved golden saxifrage and wild garlic grow. Here and there are patches of aspen, a wild service tree or two, oak, sweet chestnut and elm.

Bluebells, wood anemones and primroses cover the woodland floor in different parts of the wood, especially in the areas that have been coppiced recently.

Main entrance about a mile down a minor road leaving the A1124 (Colchester–Halstead) between Earls Colne and White Colne, heading south. It can also be entered from the north via a footpath running south from the A1124 at White Colne to Chalkney Mill.

Bus services between Colchester and Halstead run along the A1124.

Accessible at all times.

Late March through to May for spring flowers and birdsong.

Recently coppiced small-leaved lime
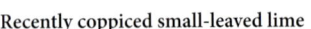

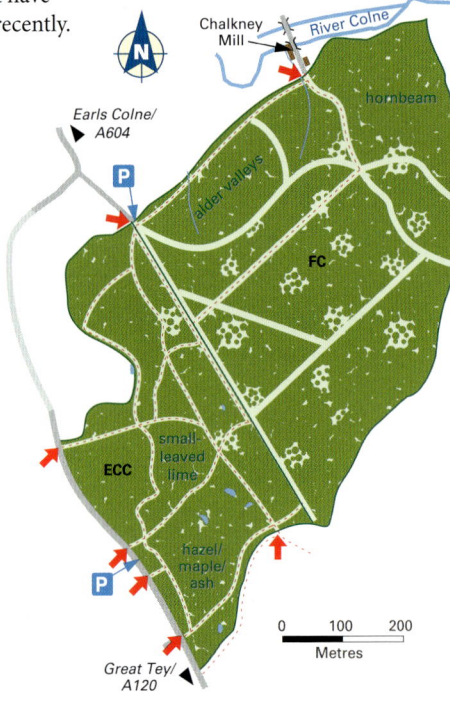

Ancient woods 17

A bluebell glade

Spring flowers

Hazel and sweet chestnut coppice

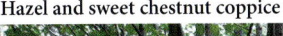

Daws Heath woods

The ancient woodlands in and around Daws Heath are all 'working woods', coppiced for centuries to supply wood for a range of purposes, and they all occupy land that was unattractive for agriculture – gravelly slopes or plateaux of infertile soil, running down into damp stream valleys. Yet they are also very different from one another, showing what effect man's treatment of a wood can have on its wildlife and character, even many decades after.

Little Haven

104ac/42ha   SS7 2LH   TQ 811 889

This nature reserve surrounding Little Haven children's hospice comprises 14 meadows, a network of fine old hedgerows and two woods.

Wyburns Wood contains a wide range of trees and plants, implying ancient origins. It is very damp in places and here it supports a type of woodland known as plateau alder, which has male fern and pendulous sedge growing underneath.

Starvelarks Wood is mainly sweet chestnut and is probably a 19th-century plantation.

The meadows are cut for hay and grazed, and in summer support many butterflies, including marbled whites.

Turn south off the A127 at Rayleigh Weir on to Rayleigh Road (A129) and turn left on to Daws Heath Road at the Woodmans Arms PH.

Hourly bus service exc. Sundays serves Daws Heath Road. More frequent services run along Rayleigh Road and pass Woodmans Arms.

Accessible at all times.

April to June for spring flowers and woodland birdsong

Wheelchair access gate to Little Haven opposite Ann's mini-market.

Please keep dogs on leads when there is livestock on Little Haven.

Tile Wood

16ac/6ha   SS7 2UN   TQ 816 890

Tile Wood is an ancient woodland joining Little Haven to Pound Wood. The tree species are predominately sessile oak, hornbeam and sweet chestnut, with some wild service. It is rich in ancient woodland plants, including wood sorrel and bluebell, and has many wood ant mounds.

West Wood

79.4ac/32ha   SS7 3YB   TQ 805 880

West Wood has been managed as coppice woodland for at least two hundred years, except that a large area of the northern part was clear felled in the 1930s, removing the standards as well as the coppice. Here the trees are oak, hornbeam, sweet chestnut and birch, with bracken and some heather beneath.

In the south of the wood there are many large oaks, with hornbeam in the wetter parts, and quite a few rowan and wild service trees.

The canalised Prittle Brook flows through from west to east, bordered by sallow, birch and ash, a pond or two and some wetland vegetation.

Access from Rayleigh Road (A129), or walk in from Daws Heath Road via Valerie Wells Wood.

Frequent bus services along Rayleigh Road.

Accessible at all times.

April to June for spring flowers and woodland birdsong.

Pound Wood

55ac/22ha **SS7 2UR** **TQ 816 888**

Pound Wood's complex geology gives it a great variation in woodland types. Sweet chestnut and birch occur on the plateaux and ridges, hornbeam and holly on the slopes, and hornbeam, ash, willow, aspen and hazel in the three stream valleys. In places there are many wild service trees. The oaks are mostly sessile, with pedunculate in the valleys.

There are fine early mediæval woodbanks, several ponds and many dells.

Bramble, bracken and bluebell dominate the woodland floor, with common cow-wheat, yellow archangel, wood spurge and figwort in the open areas.

Heath fritillaries are best seen in the open woodland under the power lines.

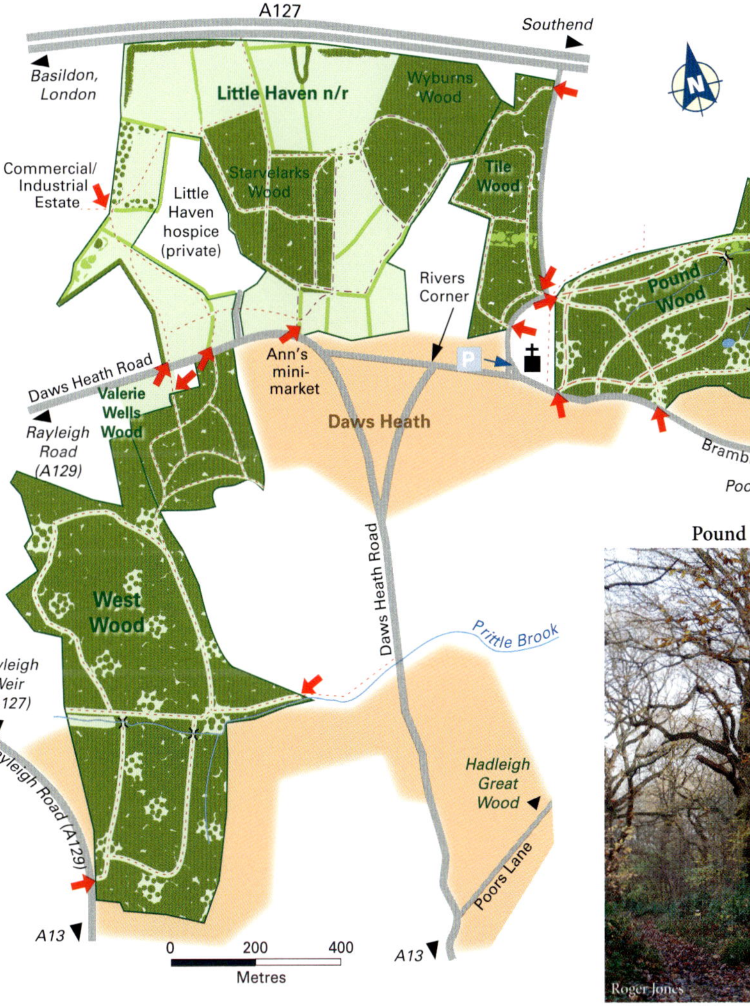

Pound Wood in autumn

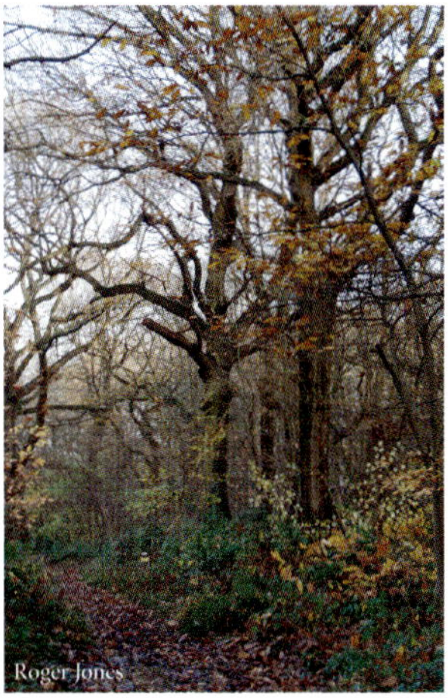

Ancient woods

Daws Heath woods Belfairs Park

447ac/181ha **SS9 4LR** *TQ 820 875* **LNR, SSSI (part)**

Southend-on-Sea Borough Council

Belfairs Park contains two large areas of ancient woodland. In the 1930s Hadleigh Great Wood was saved from destruction for housing following a local campaign. Belfairs Wood to the east was not so fortunate, because fairways were bulldozed through it to construct a golf course.

Hadleigh Great Wood has a history of many centuries of uninterrupted coppicing, and a wide range of flowers and shrubs grow among the trees, including sheets of wood anemones.

The canopy trees are mainly oak and sweet chestnut, and it also has significant numbers of alder buckthorn trees, foodplant of brimstone butterfly caterpillars. Here and there you can see patches of ling heather.

As well as brimstone and heath fritillary, white admiral and marbled white butterflies can be seen here in summer.

Belfairs Wood has not had the same level of management and is more heavily shaded and much poorer in wildlife. It is a good place to see nuthatch and woodpeckers, and has many paths and small clearings frequented by butterflies.

The Prittle Brook enters from the west, then flows

Brimstone *flies April–May and August–September*

Ancient woods

down the south-western fringe of Belfairs Wood. Although heavily shaded, it has a natural channel lined here and there with aquatic plants.

There is a Woodland Centre on the fringe of Belfairs Wood, managed by Essex Wildlife Trust, showcasing woodland management.

Access from Eastwood Road North, reached from the A13 via Eastwood Road and from the A127 westbound via The Fairway.

Regular bus services between Basildon and Southend run along the A13 to the south.

Accessible at all times. Car park open dawn to dusk. Woodland Centre open daily 10am–5pm (4pm in winter) exc. Xmas Day and Boxing Day.

May for woodland flowers and birdsong, and mid-June to mid-July for woodland butterflies.

Dogs permitted in Belfairs Park but not inside the Woodland Centre.

Prittle Brook

Coppice clearing in Hadleigh Great Wood

Ancient woods

Hillhouse Wood

34ac/13.4ha   **CO6 3DU**   **TL 945 280**

This ancient woodland near Colchester, is a light and open woodland with many glades and an open canopy of mainly oak and ash trees. The hazel growing beneath them is being coppiced in the traditional manner by local volunteers. It was acquired by the Woodland Trust with help from Colchester Council and a local appeal. In spring the wood is carpeted with bluebells and wood anemones. Its birdlife includes resident woodpeckers, with blackcap, nightingale and garden warbler visiting in summer. It also has a colony of white-letter hairstreak butterflies.

Just north of West Bergholt, reached from the end of Hall Road, which runs east from the B1508 (Colchester–Sudbury). Parking space for a few cars at the end of Hall Road.

Buses between Colchester and Sudbury run along the B1508.

Accessible at all times.

Spring for woodland flowers and birdsong.

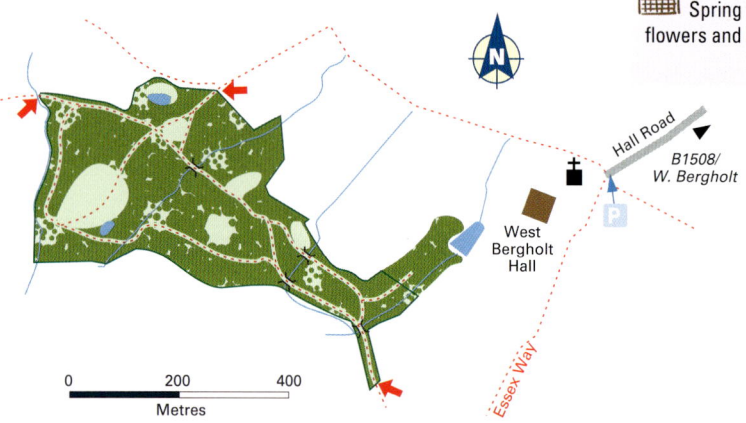

White-letter hairstreak
flies July–August
Ken Wooldridge

Ancient woods   23

Woodland birds

These are the birds you are most likely to encounter in woodland, over and above those that you will often see in gardens as well, such as blackbirds, chaffinches and great and blue tits

Blackcap *male (female has a brown cap), a summer visitor with a clear flute-like song*
Alan Williams

Chiffchaff *another widespread summer visitor, named after its monotonous two-note song*
Andreas Trepte

Nuthatch *resident; walks down tree trunks as well as up, looking for insects and grubs*
David Harrison

Great spotted woodpecker *resident; drums on trees to hold territory and maintain contact with its mate*
Alan Williams

Treecreeper *resident; walks up trees picking insects and spiders from the bark*
Mick Lobb

Ancient woods

Hockley Woods

270ac/109ha   **SS5 4RQ**   **TQ 833 924**   **SSSI**

If you only have time to visit one ancient woodland then Hockley Woods is the best choice. It is the largest continuous native woodland in the whole of eastern England, consisting of a group of half-a-dozen ancient woods, virtually intact except for a few bits lost around the fringes.

It is not as rich in wild flowers as some of the northern Essex woods, but has a wide variety of woodland types all on one site and many ancient woodland plants. It is crisscrossed by woodbanks, some dating from the Middle Ages.

The ground falls steeply from the car park with a variety of trees on the upper slopes including oak, sweet chestnut, ash and rowan. These give way to oak, hornbeam and hazel on the heavier and wetter soils lower down, where the trees are being coppiced in patches and along the broad rides.

The heath fritillary butterfly has been reintroduced here and large patches of its foodplant, common cow-wheat, grow alongside the rides and among the recently coppiced trees. The best place to see the butterflies is along the broad rides across the southern section in the south and east, which are kept open by regular coppicing and lined with common cow-wheat and wood ant mounds.

Common cow-wheat *fl. June–August*
Chris Gibson

Ancient woods

South of the B1013 Rayleigh-to-Rochford road, just west of Hockley. The Bull Inn is right next to the entrance road.

Hockley station is about 20 minutes' walk. Bus services from Rayleigh and Southend run past the main entrance.

Accessible at all times.

May for early flowers and birdsong; mid-June to mid-July for heath fritillaries, and later in summer for flying insects and wild flowers along the rides.

Wood ant mound surrounded by common cow-wheat

Ride in Hockley Woods

Norsey Wood

165ac/66ha **CM11 1HA** **TQ 691 955** **SSSI, LNR**

Norsey Wood is mixed coppice woodland, at least part of it continuously wooded since Roman times, and is criss-crossed by ancient woodbanks and ditches. It lies on gravelly deposits on top of London Clay, so the vegetation varies greatly from a well-drained plateau down to the damper and heavier soils in the southern valleys.

On the plateau is mainly sweet chestnut coppice, with occasional colonies of heather and, not far from the visitor centre, some massive stools of coppiced hornbeam that must be at least 500 years old. In the marshy valleys, you will find alder, ash and willow coppice, with areas of pendulous sedge and buckler fern.

It has one of the greatest concentrations of bluebells in Britain and large numbers of hard fern. Water violet, bog bean and skullcap grow in and around the ponds.

Roger Jones

- On Norsey Road, which turns off the B1007 just north of Billericay centre.
- About 10 minutes' walk from Billericay rail station.
- Site and car park open at all times; visitor centre weekends only.
- April–May for bluebells and songbirds; October for fungi.

Ancient woods 27

Oxlip woods

Oxlips grow only in ancient woods in the area where the counties of Essex, Cambridgeshire and Suffolk meet. This is an area of boulder clay soils, which are very chalky and produce woods that are unusually complex, with a wide variety of plants. Here are three of the best oxlip woods in Uttlesford, the north-west corner of Essex.

Rowney Wood

204ac/82ha   **CB10 2YA**   **TL 574 338**

This large ancient wood was planted up with conifers in the 1950s but has now mostly been returned to native deciduous woodland. It is being coppiced regularly.

The wide rides are lined with wild flowers in summer, including ragged robin, red campion and bugle. It also has some wet, open areas with sedges and ferns.

It has purple emperor and white-letter hairstreak butterflies and many deer.

Turn south off the B184 (Thaxted–Saffron Walden) west of Rowney Corner and park in layby near Carver Barracks.

Hourly buses Saffron Walden–Stansted Airport serve Debden: 800m walk via Harcamlow Way.

Accessible at all times.

Circular route usable by wheelchairs in all but the worst weather conditions.

Ragged robin *flowers May–July*

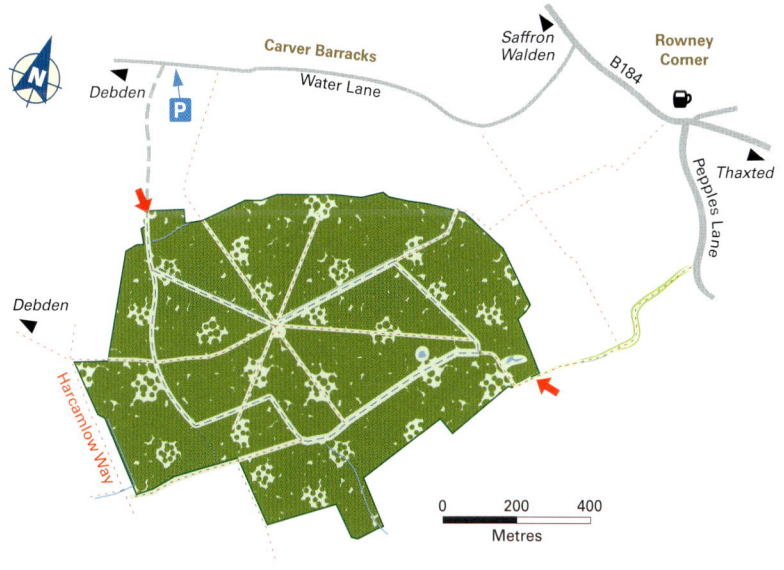

Oxlip woods Shadwell Wood

17.5ac/7ha   CB10 2HJ   TL 573 412   SSSI

The dominant trees in this delightful small wood are oak and ash, with coppiced hazel and maple growing beneath them. It also has midland hawthorns, rare trees such as lineage elm and bird cherry, and *Daphne mezereum*, popular for the garden but rare in the wild.

A host of flowering plants grow on the woodland floor. Early spring brings oxlips, wood violets and wood anemones. These give way to early purple orchids, bluebells, bugle and herb paris. Summer brings common spotted orchids, meadowsweet and sanicle.

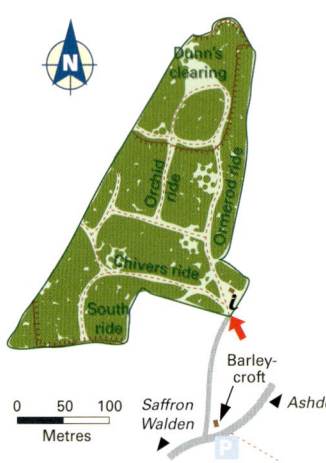

On the main road from Saffron Walden, about one mile before the village of Ashdon. Entrance on foot by a track at the side of 'Barleycroft' bungalow. Park in the layby opposite.

Accessible at all times.

Spring through to early summer for flowers and migrant birds.

Please keep your dog on a lead and keep deer gates shut.

Sanicle *flowers May–June*

Ancient pollard in Shadwell Wood

Ancient woods

West Wood

58ac/23ha   **CB10 2SA**   **TL 624 332**   **SSSI**

This mixed deciduous wood near Thaxted is one of the finest in the area. On chalky boulder clay, it has a history of coppicing dating back to the middle ages.

As well as oxlips it has early purple and greater butterfly orchids, and also wood barley, which is rare in Essex. Pendulous sedge grows along the rides.

Nesting birds include goldcrest, several migrant warblers, stock dove and buzzard. Butterflies include speckled wood, brimstone and ringlet.

Four ponds support great crested newts as well as many dragonflies and damselflies.

 On the B1051 midway between Thaxted and Great Sampford, one mile north-east of Thaxted. A track leads to the reserve entrance from the western side of the road.

Accessible at all times.

Early spring through to mid-summer for flowers and breeding birds.

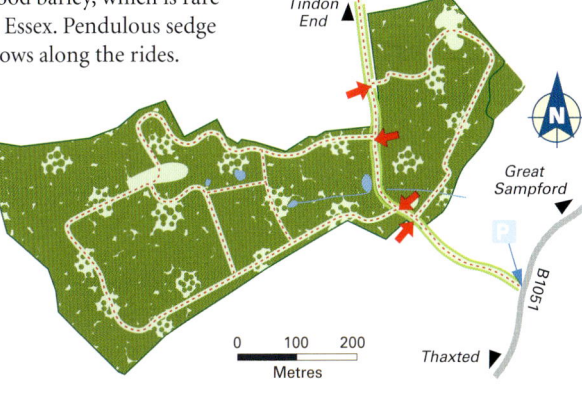

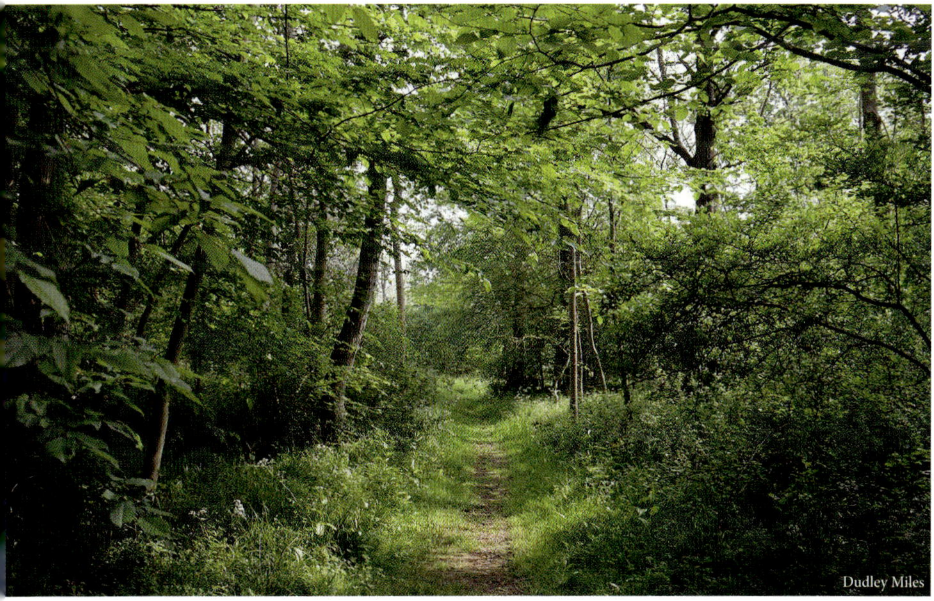

Dudley Miles

Parndon Woods & Common

129ac/52ha   CM19 4SF   TL 444 072   LNR, SSSI (part)

Parndon Wood, an ancient woodland on Harlow's southern ridge, consists mainly of hornbeam coppice with oak standards. Coppicing lapsed after World War II but has been resumed to encourage woodland plants and animals. The wood is visited by deer and fencing has to be used to prevent them from damaging the newly coppiced trees.

It was bought by Harlow Council in 1968 to become a Local Nature Reserve. In 2004 the reserve was extended to include Parndon Common and two more ancient woods to the west.

Parndon Common is cut annually for hay and before the hay cut provides a good show of yellow rattle, common spotted orchids and cowslips. It has occasional mature oaks.

Hospital and Risden's Woods are mainly coppiced hornbeam and oak, like Parndon Wood, plus some large ash in the wetter southern part. Coppicing has been resumed here also.

Bats are a special feature. Pipistrelles, the smallest British bats, are the commonest, and daubenton's and brown long-eared bats can be seen here also.

Access via Parndon Wood Road, on the southern fringe of Harlow. From the A414 follow signs to Parndon Wood Crematorium and park on the right just past the crematorium entrance. The entrance to Parndon Wood is through the green gates next on the right. The rest of the site can be reached via the public footpath near the crematorium entrance.

All except Parndon Wood accessible at all times. Parndon Wood is closed on Mondays and Tuesdays, and otherwise opens for varying times from 11am – check the Harlow Council website for details.

One hide in Parndon Wood accessible by wheelchairs via a boardwalk.

Dogs are not allowed into Parndon Wood.

Yellow rattle *flowers mid-May–July*
Owen Keen

Ancient woods

Shut Heath Wood

50ac/20ha   CM8 3ED   TL 853 133

This Essex Wildlife Trust reserve, just below the crest of the Great Totham Ridge, includes 23 acres of ancient woodland forming part of the Chantry Wood complex. The remaining 27 acres are arable land managed by a tenant farmer.

The wood comprises large oak standards with sections of sweet chestnut and hornbeam coppice, with an underwood of ash, elder and hazel. The eastern edge is wet, with an open glade and thick scrub areas, while the southern edge consists of secondary woodland of silver birch and hawthorn that has colonised the adjacent field edges. The Trust has resumed coppicing and created some open areas to rejuvenate the wood.

In spring, bugle, cuckoo flower, wood sorrel, bluebells, wood anemone, primrose and dog violet flower, followed in summer by yellow pimpernel, red bartsia, greater birdsfoot trefoil and wood sage.

Dragonflies and damselflies may be seen in the glade and, in July, glow-worms. There is lots of standing dead wood here which is valuable for invertebrates, and especially wood ants.

Leave the B1022 at Roundbush Corner, Great Totham, taking Mountains Road. After about 1200m take the first turning on the right (Tiptree Road), and the entrance is about 400m down on the left with double gates at the entrance. Take care when leaving as visibility is restricted.

Bus to Great Totham from Maldon or Colchester and get off at Great Totham post office. The reserve is 800m north.

Accessible at all times.

March and April for spring flowers.

Recently coppiced area at Shut Heath Wood

Red bartsia flowers June–August

Ancient woods

Stour Estuary

This section of the estuary of the River Stour to the west of Harwich has saltmarsh and intertidal mudflats adjoining ancient woodland – the only place in Essex where you can see this. Copperas Bay is nationally important for wading birds such as black-tailed godwit, dunlin and redshank and, together with Stour Wood, forms the RSPB's Stour Estuary reserve. Essex Wildlife Trust owns another ancient woodland alongside the bay, Copperas Wood.

Stour Wood

135ac/54ha   CO12 5ND   TM 192 311   SSSI

Stour Wood is one of the best ancient sweet chestnut woods in Essex. It was worked as coppice until the 1970s and coppicing has been resumed by RSPB on a long (20-year) cycle. It has a mixture of trees apart from sweet chestnut, including a few surviving small-leaved lime and many field maple on the edge of the wood.

It has some unusual flowers, including sweet woodruff and early purple orchid.

It is full of birdsong in spring and early summer. Later in summer look out for white admiral and silver-washed fritillary butterflies.

Sweet woodruff *fl. April–May*

Early purple orchid *fl. April–June*

Ancient woods

Copperas Wood

34.3ac/14ha   **CO12 5NE**   **TM 199 312**   **SSSI**

This ancient wood consists mainly of coppiced sweet chestnut and hornbeam. Coppicing has produced carpets of bluebell, yellow archangel and red campion. Among other flowering plants are moschatel, climbing corydalis, and a few sweet woodruff and vervain. The wood is rich in ferns, and in particular soft shield fern.

North of the B1352 between the villages of Wrabness and Ramsey. Stour Wood is signposted from the road; Copperas Wood is 300m down the Essex Way, beside a large white flat-roofed house.

Stour Wood is about 800m walk from Wrabness station via a public footpath. Buses from Colchester to Harwich via Wrabness run along the B1352.

Accessible at all times.

May and June for wild flowers and birdsong; summer for butterflies in Stour Wood; autumn and winter for good views of the birds in Copperas Bay.

Wheelchair trail in Stour Wood.

Yellow archangel fl. May–June

Path in Copperas Wood

Ancient woods

Weeleyhall Wood

78ac/31ha   **CO16 9AT**   *TM 156 212*   *SSSI*

ESSEX Wildlife Trust

One of the finest surviving woods in Tendring, although it suffered severely in the 1987 storm. Standard oaks provide most of the timber but there are about eight acres of sweet chestnut coppice, a similar area of scots and corsican pine plantation, an area of hazel coppice, and alder glades with an important ground flora that includes moschatel.

In spring the bluebells (which carpet almost half the wood), yellow archangel and climbing corydalis make a fine display. Several fern species are also to be found.

The wood has good numbers of woodland birds, including nightingales.

Reached from the B1441 (Colchester to Clacton) via Church Lane. Park in front of Weeley Church. Access to the wood is down a private track just past the pond.

Several bus services to/from Clacton run along the B1441. Or train to Weeley and more than a mile walk each way.

Accessible at all times

May for early flowers and breeding birds.

Please keep dogs on a lead down the track across farmland and under strict control within the wood.

Moschatel *aka Town Hall Clock*
Bernd Haynold

Early morning in the wood
Glyn Baker

Grassland and heath
Where have all the flowers gone?

Flower-rich grassland is a fundamental component of the natural world, providing resources that a wide variety of insects and other invertebrates depend on. These in turn provide valuable services such as pollination and serve as food for many other animals higher up the food chain. Without flowering plants our ecosystem would be seriously weakened and would very probably collapse.

97% loss since WWII

Natural vegetation for most of lowland England is woodland. To create grassland you have to get rid of the trees and then graze or cut the vegetation regularly to prevent them from moving back in again.

In England previous generations did this to grow crops and grass to feed their livestock. They created permanent pastures and hay meadows that never saw a sack of artificial fertiliser, and as a result nutrient levels were low. This allowed the flowering plants to compete with vigorous grasses, creating flower-rich grasslands that now we rarely see anywhere except in nature reserves.

Artificial fertilisers and powerful farm machinery have put an end to them, and the figure often quoted for the loss of these flower-rich grasslands since World War II is 97%.

Tom Heenan

Grassland and heath

Heaths and commons

As well as farmed countryside, Essex also had large areas of heath. Heaths developed on infertile, free-draining soils and were a rich mosaic of heather, gorse, bracken, flowers and grasses. From the 18th century on, heath was steadily lost to agriculture and, more recently, to housing and other development. As grazing and other uses declined, trees moved into most of the remaining heaths and they reverted to scrub and woodland.

Trees shade out most of the flowering plants and also, over time, their falling leaves break down in the soil and raise nutrient levels. As a result, recovering a scrubbed-over heath can be a laborious business, involving scraping off the topsoil and removing thousands of tree seedlings.

Cattle grazing on recovered heath in Epping Forest

The largest intact heath in Essex is at Tiptree, and elsewhere fragments of heath have survived or been recovered, such as in parts of Epping Forest and around Danbury.

The other place where flower-rich grassland has survived is on common land, where local people grazed their livestock and exploited the vegetation for bedding, fuel and other purposes. Grazing kept the commons open until the early 1900s, after which most filled up with trees and scrub. A few have survived and these, such as at Harlow, Danbury and Galleywood, are being managed for wildlife.

Managing grasslands

Grassland has to be managed by cutting or grazing to prevent it from suffering the same fate as many heaths and commons. The traditional way is to cut for hay in summer then graze with cattle, although often cutting is the only practical option.

In the past, grasslands in public parks have been *over*-managed by frequent cutting which drives out all but the grasses and a few low-growing wild flowers. Now, though, many parks are being managed more sensitively, so you can also find good grasslands in the Parkland section (p.81).

Heather on Lingwood Common, surrounded by a mass of birch seedlings

Grassland and heath

Curtismill Green

Brentwood Borough Council

119ac/48ha   RM4 1HP   TQ 517 965   SSSI

This area of common land surrounds Willow Cottage, with an open-air theatre nearby. Although the M25 is audible not far away, once there you could be in another age, when horses were the main form of transport.

In the north it is open grassland with clumps of dense scrub and scattered oaks, grazed by horses. The soils are a mixture of London clay and chalky boulder clay, in places damp, elsewhere dry, and as a result it supports some unusual plants, including betony, lesser spearwort, pepper saxifrage and sneezewort.

As you walk south the trees become denser, consisting mainly of mature oaks with a scattering of hornbeam, hawthorn and holly, and with a brook running through them. In spring and summer the woods are full of speckled wood butterflies.

Speckled wood *flies April–Sept.*

Access from the north via Albyns lane, which leaves the roundabout where the B175 joins the A113, about a mile east of Abridge; or via footpaths and byroads from the minor road between Stapleford Abbotts and Navestock Heath. Parking is difficult, so either get someone to drop you off or walk or cycle in.

Accessible at all times

May for early flowers and birdsong in the woods; July–August for meadow flowers and insects.

The paths are used heavily by horses, so are pockmarked and rutted: wear good boots and beware wet patches in winter.

Open air theatre at Curtismill Green

Grassland and heath

Danbury

Danbury is fortunate in still being surrounded by several fine areas of common and heath. These had been heavily invaded by trees and scrub, but the conservation organisations that manage them now – the National Trust and Essex Wildlife Trust – have been working hard to rehabilitate them. In the areas that they have tackled, heathland plants have recolonised, and with an effort of the imagination you can visualise what they must have looked like in their prime.

Danbury Common

218ac/87ha   CM3 4JH   TL 781 041   SSSI

This is a typical ancient common, criss-crossed by roads, tracks and paths, with long straggling boundaries funnelling out along the roads, and with houses in enclaves.

Much of the southern part is original open common. Parts of it are mown at different heights and times throughout the year and have retained many heathland plants.

The northern part has reverted to woodland.

Danbury Common

The Backwarden

30ac/12ha   CM3 4JH   TL 781 041   SSSI

This part of the common has a great variety of habitats for its size – a number of pools and bogs, areas of restored heath, a small marsh, blackthorn thickets, and both old and secondary woodland, including some aspen groves.

The result is a wide variety of flowers, including heathland species such as tormentil and heath milkwort, and wetland species like marsh willowherb, pennywort and common and lesser skullcap.

Nesting birds include nightingale, blackcap and woodpeckers. Insects include green hairstreak butterflies and green tiger beetles. Many brimstone butterflies appear in spring because of the alder buckthorn trees, foodplant of its caterpillars.

Green hairstreak
flies mid-May–June

Grassland and heath

On both sides of Bicknacre Road, which runs south from Danbury. Turn off the A414 at Eve's Corner and follow Penny Royal Road to Bicknacre Road.

Chelmsford–Maldon bus to Eve's Corner. (Chelmsford–S. Woodham Ferrers bus passes the common.)

Accessible at all times.

May for birdsong; July–September for heathland plants; July for glow-worms.

Please keep dogs under control and on leads when livestock are present.

Hitchcock's Meadows

15ac/6ha   CM3 4FJ   TL 788 049   SSSI

On hilly land adjoining Danbury Common, much of this is flower-rich ancient meadows and the rest is secondary woodland, scrubland and marsh.

The meadows are grazed to keep them open and are rich in wild flowers, including agrimony, knapweed and green-winged orchids, as well as less usual plants such as eyebright, common milkwort and autumn lady's tresses.

The marsh is dominated by the bright emerald green of giant horsetail, with a patch of devilsbit scabious.

The hedgerows and thickets attract a good number of bird species and the reserve is rich in insect life, including glow-worms.

Danbury Danbury Ridge

250ac/100ha   CM3 4NZ   TL 775 064   SSSI (part)

The Danbury Ridge reserves are a patchwork of former common and heath, woodland, streams and bogs. In reality there is much more woodland than grassland, but it does illustrate what has happened to many heaths and commons, and it is full of interest and always worth a visit, whatever you prefer.

Woodham Walter Common, a gravel-covered plateau sloping down to stream valleys on both sides, is principally secondary woodland, with a few areas and some rides that are being kept open to encourage low-growing plants, and especially ling heather. It is noted for its sessile oak trees, with many rowan and a scattering of wild service and alder buckthorn.

Little Baddow Heath too is mainly secondary woodland, descending steeply to a stream valley containing primrose, fen bedstraw and ragged robin. A section to the north has been restored and here can be found many wild flowers, including unusual plants such as heath milkwort and goldenrod.

Poors Piece sits in the angle to the west of Little Baddow Heath. It contains many oak pollards, implying that it was once used as wood-pasture. In its southern corner is a marsh full of wetland plants, and notably hemp agrimony and lady fern.

Birch Wood at its northern corner consists mainly of hornbeam coppice, worked on a 20-year cycle.

Pheasanthouse Wood to the west is mixed woodland with a raised bog. This has dense hummocks of sphagnum moss and large numbers of the rare lesser skullcap.

Scrubs Wood to the south consists mainly of hornbeam and chestnut coppice with oak standards, plus some wild service trees.

Dormice, once common but now much reduced in numbers, are found in many parts of the reserve. The birdlife includes nuthatch, woodpeckers, migrant warblers and, intermittently, nightingale. There are good numbers of butterflies including brimstone, ringlet and small copper.

Lily-of-the-valley is a special feature of Danbury Ridge, and other unusual wild flowers here include yellow archangel, greater butterfly orchid and sanicle.

Footbridge in Danbury Ridge

Grassland and heath   41

Lily-of-the-valley *flowers in May*

Winter stream

Foot access from the west via Firtree Lane, off The Ridge; from the east via Common Lane, Woodham Walter; and from the south via Twitty Fee or Runsell Lane, a turning to the right 600m along Little Baddow Road from Eve's Corner.

Regular bus services Chelmsford–Maldon and Chelmsford–S. Woodham Ferrers. Get off at Eve's Corner.

Accessible at all times.

May for breeding birds and wild flowers; June for ferns and bog plants and for butterflies; autumn for fungi.

Please keep dogs on leads when crossing Pheasanthouse Farm.

Grassland and heath

Galleywood Common

60ac/24ha   *CM2 8JS*   *TL 704 025*   *LNR*

This fine piece of common land a couple of miles south of Chelmsford is a typical common in its irregular shape, including several enclaves containing buildings, and in the many pits and depressions, probably the result of commoners digging out gravel in the past.

It packs a great variety of habitats into a relatively small space. These include lowland heath, ponds, mire, marsh, grassland, bracken-covered areas and woodland.

Unusual plants growing here include star sedge, lesser skullcap and heath spotted orchid.

Leave the A12 at its junction with the B1007 and turn north towards Galleywood and Chelmsford.

Buses from Chelmsford to Basildon, Billericay and Wickford run down the B1007 past the common.

Accessible at all times.

Heath spotted orchid fl. June–July
Jim Champion

Typical heathland on Galleywood Common

Grassland and heath   43

Harlow & Latton Commons

124ac/50ha   **CM17 9ND**   **TL 480 080**

These are two large areas of common land on the south-eastern fringe of Harlow, either side of the A414 and linked by a pedestrian underpass. They are mainly open grassland, parts of which are grazed by horses and parts cut for hay, so have a diversity of wild flowers.

On Harlow Common there are patches of woodland, one just east of the A414 and another surrounding the lake. The southern fringe of Latton Common is wooded also, mainly oak.

There is a network of footpaths, including the Forest Way long-distance path that runs all the way through from west to east.

Access from Latton Common Road, reached from the A414 northbound by turning right (then via Potter Street) or left (then via Trotters Road) respectively at the roundabout where the A414 meets Southern Way (A1169), i.e. the first roundabout north of M11 junction 7.

Frequent buses ex. Sundays from Harlow Town stn.

Accessible at all times.

Summer for wild flowers and for dragonflies around the lake and ponds.

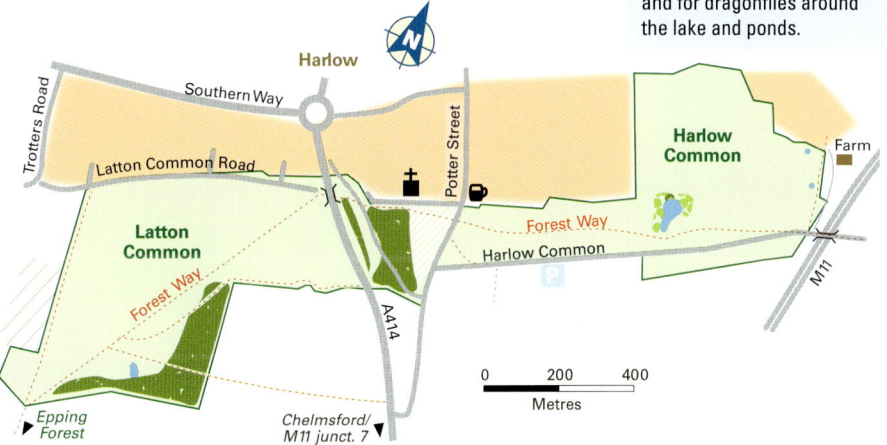

Latton Common
Glyn Baker

Hunsdon Mead

68ac/27ha   *CM19 5EH*   *TL 421 114*   *SSSI*

This area of common land between the River Stort and the Stort Navigation is one of the finest surviving areas of unimproved grassland in eastern England. For over 600 years it has been managed on the ancient Lammas system, under which it is grazed in late summer after a July hay cut.

It provides a superb display of flowering plants. In April and May it is yellow with cowslips and marsh marigolds. As May gives way to June plants such as yellow rattle, ragged robin, cuckoo flower, meadowsweet and bugle come into flower. There are small colonies of green-winged orchid and adders-tongue fern. Quaking grass and several uncommon sedge species are present also.

In summer you can expect to see all the typical grassland butterflies and many dragonflies.

During the winter, when the Mead floods, large flocks of lapwing and golden plover come to feed along with other winter visitors.

Follow the towpath from Roydon in the direction of Harlow – a walk of about one mile. The easiest parking is at Roydon station.

Roydon station (Liverpool St–Cambridge).

Accessible at all times.

From mid-April until the end of June for flowers, and later in the summer for dragonflies and other insects.

Between March and July please do not walk across or into the Mead itself until the hay is cut.

Adderstongue fern

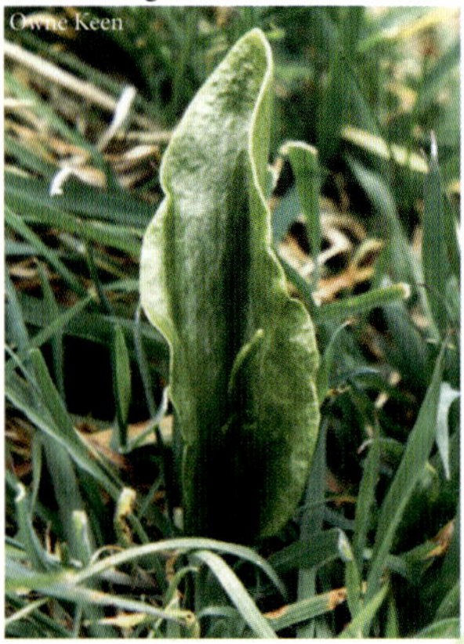

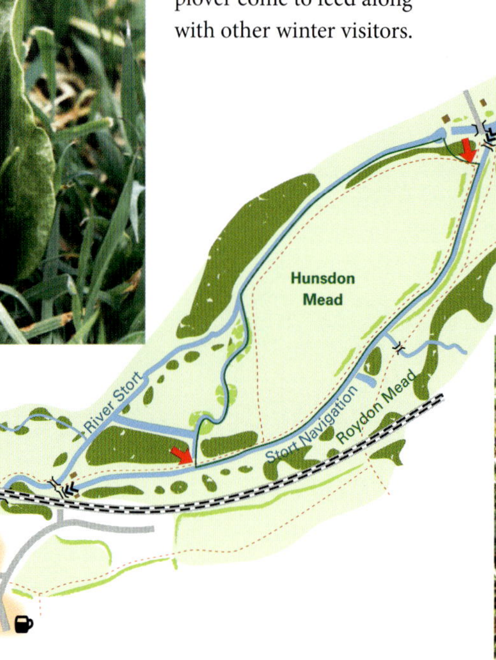

Bugle

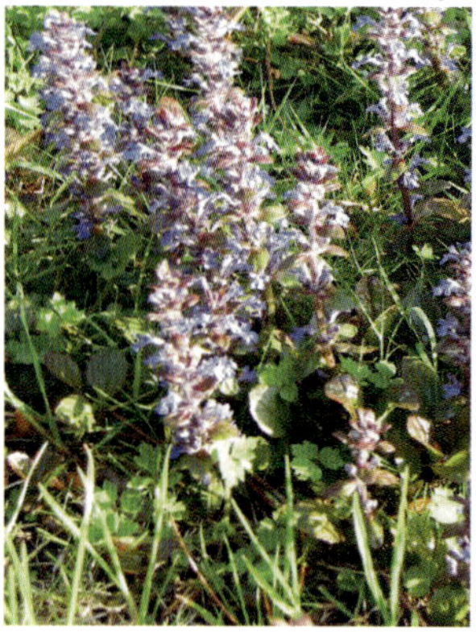

Langdon

Just south of Basildon lies a crescent-shaped hilly ridge more than 100m high, extending from the former plotland township of Dunton in the west to Vange in the east and giving tremendous views over the Thames estuary and into east London. Its name, Langdon, means 'long hill' and much of its land is set aside for wildlife and for recreation, with Essex Wildlife Trust's Langdon nature reserve to the north and west, linking with Langdon Hills country park, managed by Thurrock Council, to the south and east.

Langdon nature reserve

520ac/211ha   SS16 6EB   TQ 659 874   SSSI

This is Essex Wildlife Trust's largest inland reserve, and much of it is former plotlands, that is land divided up into small plots and sold to Londoners in the mid-20th century as their little place in the country.

The signs are still there in the grid structure of the old plotland roads and the many garden 'escapes' – plants from the original gardens that have managed to survive. There is also an original plotland house near the Dunton visitor centre that has been preserved as a museum.

Langdon has acres of flower-rich meadows, plus ponds, ancient and secondary woodland, and hundreds of former plotland gardens.

The original reserve consisted of four sections: from west to east these are Dunton, Lincewood, Marks Hill and Willow Park. In 2007 the reserve was extended to include a large lake and some meadows immediately north of Dunton now called (unsurprisingly) *Langdon Lake & Meadows*.

Between the A127 and the A13 4.5 miles east of M25 junction 29. Signposted by brown signs from the north from the B148 turning off the A127, and from the south from the A13.

Laindon station on the Fenchurch Street–Southend line is less than 800m from the reserve. Frequent bus services run from Basildon town centre to Laindon station, to Langdon Hills and to Highview Avenue.

Reserve accessible at all times. Dunton visitor centre open 9am – 5pm (4pm in winter).

Spring for breeding birds and early flowers such as primroses; summer for orchids and other flowers; autumn for fruit and berries and for late butterflies.

Multi-use paths (horses and bikes) throughout.

Flower-rich grassland in Willow Park

Langdon (continued)

Langdon Lake & Meadows

This is former plotlands and agricultural land on the west side of the Langdon Hills ridge. It has a large lake, meadows and broadleaved woodland.

The meadows are particularly important for grizzled skipper butterflies, now very scarce, and are being managed to suit them.

It also attracts a variety of birds, including raptors such as hobby, kestrel and sparrowhawk, and little grebe, wigeon, and common tern on the lake.

Bats can be seen hunting over the lake on warm evenings.

Grizzled skipper *fl. May–mid-June*

Dunton plotlands

Here you will find the remains of plotland homes and gardens, wide grassy avenues bordered by hawthorn scrub, and glades where wild flowers compete with garden escapes.

This patchwork of habitats is ideal for butterflies. Old orchards attract animals to feed in autumn and the plotland ruins offer basking sites for snakes and lizards.

Green-winged orchid *flowers May*
Adrian Knowles

Lincewood

Lincewod has derelict plotland roads and, on higher ground, ancient and secondary woodland. Bluebells carpet the woodland floor in spring and garden escapes flower throughout the summer – goat's rue, old roses and many others. A recreation ground to the north has thousands of green-winged orchids in May.

Grassland and heath

Marks Hill

Marks Hill is a patchwork of ancient and secondary woodland, meadows and deserted plotlands. In spring the woods offer a fine display of bluebells, wood anemones and primroses, and the grassland has many common spotted orchids.

Several warbler species breed and in some years the nightingale. The boundary oaks are home to a colony of purple hairstreak butterflies.

Purple hairstreak
flies mid-July to late August

Willow Park

This was once a mediæval deer park. The flower-rich hay meadows and rough grassland are bordered by ancient hedgerows and more recent mixed plantations. Seven ponds of varying sizes attract a wide range of dragonflies and damselflies.

Langdon Langdon Hills country park

400ac/162ha *SS17 9NH* *TQ 697 861* *SSSI*

THURROCK COUNCIL

This mixture of flower-rich meadows and both ancient and more recent woodland was bought by Essex County Council in the 1930s under the Green Belt scheme and designated a country park in 1973.

Northlands, Martinhole and Hall Wood are all ancient in origin, and dominated by oak, hornbeam and ash trees. Northlands Wood also has a large number of wild service trees, a reliable sign of an ancient wood, while Hall Wood to the west has an unusual concentration of wild cherry along its western and southern fringes. Coombe Wood and The Park are former parkland, and the other woods have grown up on former farmland.

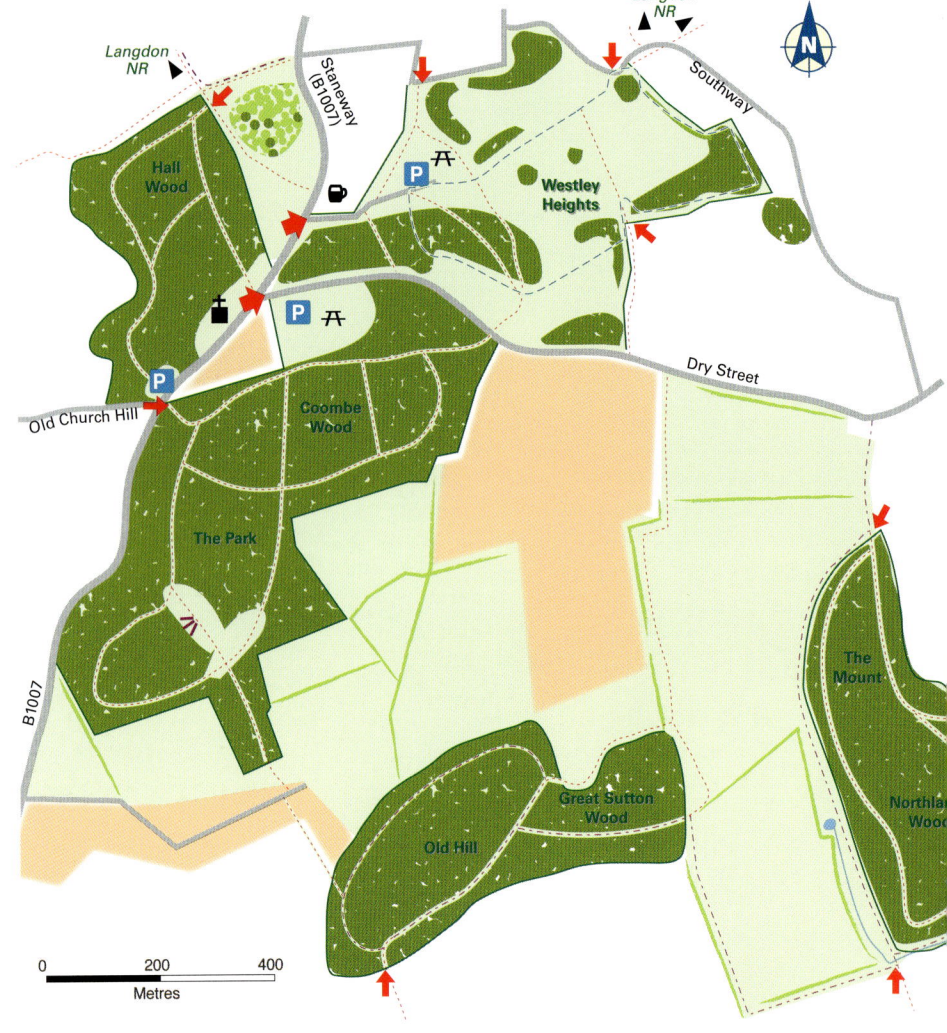

Grassland and heath 49

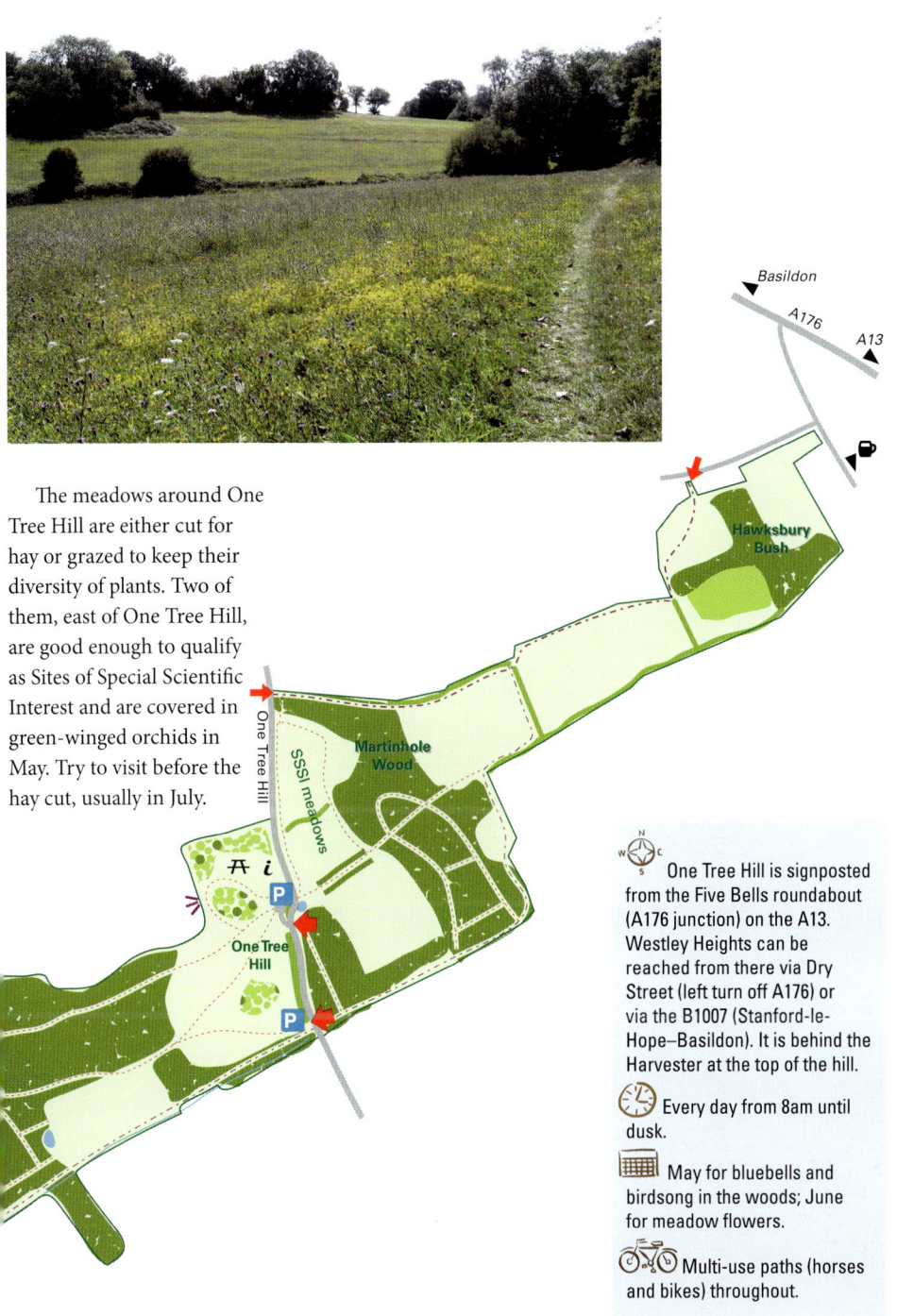

The meadows around One Tree Hill are either cut for hay or grazed to keep their diversity of plants. Two of them, east of One Tree Hill, are good enough to qualify as Sites of Special Scientific Interest and are covered in green-winged orchids in May. Try to visit before the hay cut, usually in July.

One Tree Hill is signposted from the Five Bells roundabout (A176 junction) on the A13. Westley Heights can be reached from there via Dry Street (left turn off A176) or via the B1007 (Stanford-le-Hope–Basildon). It is behind the Harvester at the top of the hill.

Every day from 8am until dusk.

May for bluebells and birdsong in the woods; June for meadow flowers.

Multi-use paths (horses and bikes) throughout.

Grassland and heath

Lower Colne Valley

As it approaches Colchester from the west the River Colne meanders across a broad flood plain, forming a green space that runs almost to the centre of the town. At its heart is Cymbeline Meadows, former farmland that Colchester Council is managing much like the ancient flood meadows that used to occupy this land. Close by are other open spaces the Council manages for wildlife – Hilly Fields and Buntings Meadow.

Cymbeline Meadows

Colchester

159ac/63.5ha   CO3 3LE   TL 980 260

This area bordering the River Colne has been farmed for hundreds of years. Now, most of it is being farmed by a tenant farmer in a wildlife-friendly way, with limited use of pesticides and features such as 'conservation headlands' – strips along the edge of arable fields sown with wild flowers that serve as reservoirs of beneficial insects.

In the north-east corner south of the railway a new wood has been planted, known as Charter Wood. Smaller woods and copses have been planted elsewhere, including beside the Colne.

The river and its bankside meadows form a wildlife corridor running through urban Colchester and they are home to kingfishers and water voles. They flood regularly in winter, encouraging wild flowers.

Water vole
Ken King

Access via public footpaths from Cymbeline Way (A133) and leading in from the north and west.

Within easy walking distance of Colchester North station.

Accessible at all times.

A parking area for disabled visitors can be reached via Baker's Lane (Spring Lane exit from the Lexden roundabout) and a surfaced pathway leads down to the river from there.

A farm trail has been laid out starting from Baker's Lane.

Grassland and heath

Hilly Fields & Buntings Meadow

40ac/16ha **CO3 3QJ** **TL 984 253**

Colchester

This public open space shares the ridge on which the town of Colchester developed, overlooking the flood plain of the River Colne. It is part of the Sheepen site that was an industrial and commercial area of Colchester in Iron Age and Roman times: most of it is a Scheduled Ancient Monument.

Since farming stopped about 40 years ago it has developed a mosaic of varied habitats. Much of it is grassland partially invaded by scrub and woodland, but the eastern section towards the town has very sandy soils and heath-like patches have developed, with broom and gorse.

At the foot of the slope against Cymbeline Way is a marsh fed by springs and a couple of ponds. Bats feed over this area.

Buntings Meadow to the west is managed particularly for butterflies and has a butterfly trail.

Accessed via Sussex Road, that runs north off Lexden Road (A1124).

Frequent bus services from Colchester Town Centre to Lexden and Stanway run along Lexden Road.

Accessible at all times.

Late spring to late summer for wild flowers and insects.

Most paths are unsuitable for wheelchairs because of the steep terrain.

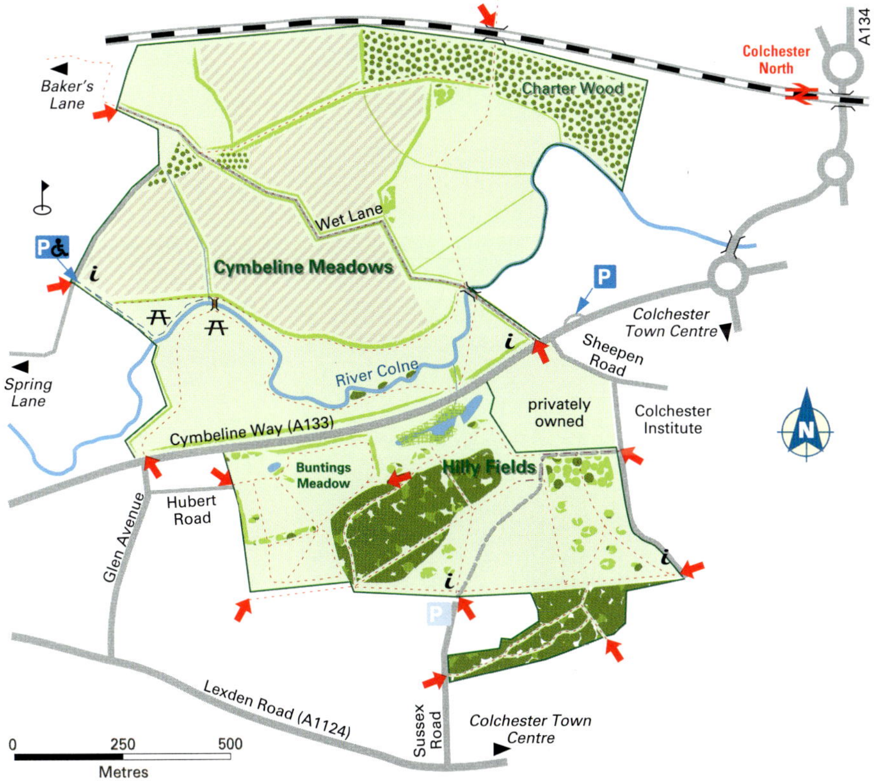

Grassland and heath

Mill Meadows

90ac/36ha   **CM12 9QQ**   *TQ 678 943*   **SSSI (part), LNR**

This large area of old meadows is not far from the centre of Billericay. They lie in rolling countryside cut by streams and ditches with occasional marshy areas. Scrub and young woodland have encroached in places but grazing by cattle is keeping much of the area open.

Stoats and foxes and many birds frequent the meadows, but it is the plant life that makes them special. There is a succession of colour from bluebells and cuckoo flower in spring, then common spotted orchids and betony, through to devilsbit scabious in late summer. It also has some plants that are scarce locally, among them harebell, ragged robin and sneezewort.

Such a range of nectar sources also attracts many butterflies and other insects.

Between Southend Road (A129) and Greens Farm Lane just south of Billericay Centre. Limited parking close by: use car parks in Billericay.

About 600m from Billericay station.

Accessible at all times.

Late spring to late summer for wild flowers and insects.

Cuckoo flower (*aka* **Lady's Smock**) *flowers April–June*

Betony *flowers July–August*

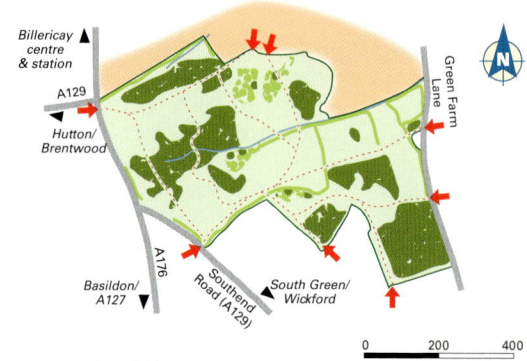

Common spotted orchid: *flowers mid-May–early August*

Devilsbit scabious *flowers July–October*

Grassland and heath

Roding Valley Meadows

158ac/63ha   *IG7 6BQ*   *TQ 430 943*   *LNR, SSSI (part)*

This is the largest surviving area of traditionally managed river-valley habitat in Essex. It consists of flower-rich hay meadows, both wet and dry, bounded by thick hedgerows, together with a small amount of scrub, secondary woodland and tree plantation. It follows the River Roding for some 1½ miles between Chigwell Lane and Roding Lane, Buckhurst Hill, as it meanders across this ancient landscape.

The meadows are managed in the traditional way by taking a hay cut in summer, after which they are grazed by longhorn cattle. They are rich in flowers, including pepper saxifrage, southern marsh orchid, ragged robin, marsh marigold and devilsbit scabious.

A green lane runs from near the river to the M11 motorway by Grange Farm. This was part of the old drovers' route from Epping Forest to Romford market, and has many woodland flowers.

Birdlife is good and varied. In spring and summer, sedge warbler, skylark, reed bunting and whitethroat can be seen about the river and meadows. Late summer sees flocks of finches and other seed-eating birds on the seed heads of thistle and teasel. Grey heron, little grebe, snipe, green and common sandpiper are regular winter visitors. Raptors about all year include little owls.

Many insects inhabit the meadows and the hedgerows, both unusual and common. Most summers produce drifts of meadow brown and other grassland butterflies.

Grassland and heath

Accessible from the Roding Valley recreation ground via a number of entrances on the Loughton side of the river. The car park is off Roding Lane, next to the David Lloyd Tennis Centre.

Buckhurst Hill, Loughton and Debden tube stations are all a lengthy walk from the reserve. Many bus services run to Debden and Loughton stations.

Accessible at all times.

For meadow flowers, any time from late spring up to the mid-July hay cut.

One-mile linear surfaced track for wheelchairs; all kissing gates adapted for wheelchairs and buggies.

Please keep dogs on leads when there is livestock on the reserve.

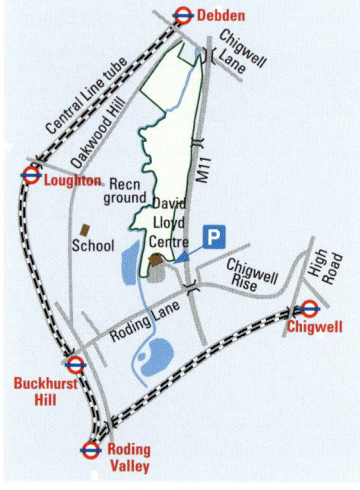

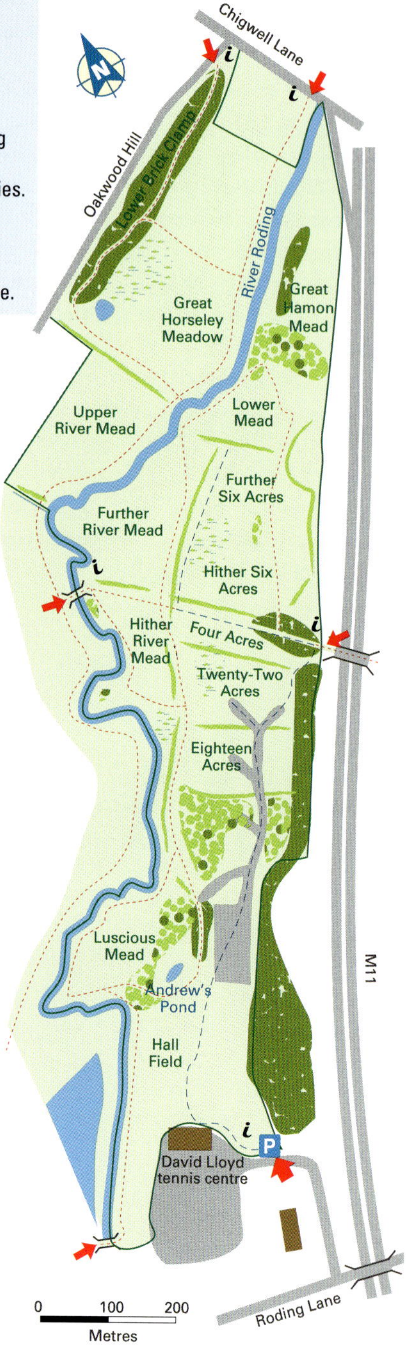

Purple loosestrife beside the Roding
Patrick Bailly

Grassland and heath 55

Tiptree Heath

60ac/24ha   **CO5 0PU**   **TL 883 147**   **SSSI**

Tiptree Heath is a small fragment of a huge heathland that used to stretch from Maldon to Messing, covering thousands of acres. It is the finest and largest area of heath in Essex, and the only place where you will find all three native heather species growing together.

After being nibbled away by enclosure for centuries, the remaining heath was ploughed up for agriculture during World War II. But it produced only poor crops, and in 1955 was sown with grass seed and left to look after itself. The result was that some of it turned into light woodland and scrub, but on large areas the heathland plants reappeared.

Recently, radical measures have been taken to restore it, including bulldozing down to the mineral soil, and some areas have been fenced off so that they can be grazed by Exmoor ponies.

Ling heather, which is tall and vigorous enough to survive in gorse, covers large areas, and there are areas of bell heather and a small amount of cross-leaved heath that prefers the wetter parts. Harebells appear in late summer, and other unusual wild plants, include heath dog-violet, allseed and chaffweed.

Its birdlife includes many willow warblers, nightingales, turtle doves and the occasional woodcock.

Turtle dove *summer visitor*
Alan Williams

The heath straddles the B1022 (Colchester–Maldon) 800m on the Maldon side of Tiptree.

Regular Maldon to Colchester bus service runs along the B1022 past the heath.

Accessible at all times.

April for acres of gorse in flower; July–September for late flowers, including the heather, and grassland butterflies.

Glyn Baker

Grassland and heath

Tylers Common

Tylers Common is an ancient common in the Metropolitan Green Belt east of Havering. Once isolated in the middle of arable farmland, now it is adjoined by Forestry Commission woodlands planted up as part of the Thames Chase Community Forest.

Tylers Common

69ac/28ha   **RM14 1TS**   **TQ 563 907**

Tylers Common is the last remaining sizeable piece of common land left in Havering. Its name derives from the brick and tile industry that exploited the clay deposits around here from Saxon times onwards.

Parts are kept open by grazing by horses and parts have been invaded by scrub and trees. In summer the open grassland is full of wild flowers, including agrimony, birdsfoot trefoil and knapweed. It also has some rarer plants, including sneezewort (in the damp south-east corner) and dwarf gorse, indicative of its heathland past.

Skylarks and meadow pipits nest here. The mix of scrub, tall hedges and open grassland also attracts seed-eating birds such as yellowhammers, linnets and bullfinches, which are in severe decline elsewhere.

There are two small ponds in which good numbers of dragonflies and amphibians breed.

Meadow pipit *partial migrant*
Alan Williams

Linnet *male, partial migrant*
Alan Williams

Bullfinch *male, resident*
Alan Williams

Grassland and heath 57

Within the triangle formed by the A127, A12 and M25 east of Harold Wood. From M25 junction 28 take the A1023 towards Brentwood and turn first right on to Nags Head Lane: the Tylers Common car park is less than a mile down on the left. Or, heading west on the A127, turn off at the first junction after the M25 and head north along Hall Lane towards Brentwood: the Pages Wood car park is on the left.

Harold Wood station is about 20 minutes' walk from Pages Wood via Harold Wood Park (see map).

Accessible at all times. Car parks open dawn to dusk.

May for breeding birds; high summer for wild flowers and insects.

Grassland and heath

Tylers Common Harold Court Woods

67ac/27ha   RM3 0LA   TQ 560 913

This substantial Forestry Commission woodland surrounding Harold Court (now residential flats) was created on former farmland. Much of it has been planted with trees, mainly native broadleaves with some scots pine and larch, adding to the surrounding tree belts, which include groups of mature black poplar and horse chestnut, and the original hedges, which include wild service trees.

Broad grassy rides and glades have been left unplanted, and these are moderately rich in flowers and provide good habitat for butterflies and small mammals.

A flower meadow and pond have been created next to the railway and there is an established pond further south.

Pages Wood

183ac/74ha   RM14 1TQ   TQ 561 894

The largest of the Forestry Commission's woodlands within Thames Chase, consisting of two former farms sloping down towards the River Ingrebourne, which is a substantial stream at this point.

At the southern end, the grazing meadows of the former Mount Pleasant Farm have been left in their original state and are rich in flowers and insects.

The former Pages Farm has been planted with groups of trees, separated by broad grassy rides and open glades.

The combination of maturing woodland with open, sunny grassland and the river makes it a good area for birds at almost any time of the year. In summer, banded demoiselles can be seen along the river and a variety of butterflies and other insects in the grassland.

Banded demoiselle
female, flies June–August

Tylers Wood

30ac/12ha   CM13 3JA   TQ 572 904

A hilltop and valley side adjoining Tylers Common, sloping down from the M25 motorway to a bridleway, and with an arm projecting northwards beside the motorway up to a footbridge. Former arable land, it is now substantially open, sunny grassland sheltered by patches of maturing native broad-leaved trees, including much birch. Flowering plants include agrimony and knapweed. It provides good habitat for butterflies and also for reptiles.

The arm projecting northwards has sheets of fleabane in late summer.

Fleabane *fl. August–September*

Forests
Hunting grounds for kings

We have William the Conqueror to thank for our forests. For him, forests were areas where Forest Law applied, meaning that the crown asserted its ownership of all the deer and the right to take them whenever the table demanded. Many forests were declared over much of England and they included open country – heathland or farmland – and, sometimes but not always, woods as well. It is mainly the forests with woods that have survived to this day.

Wood-pasture

Deer could be fenced out of woods but not out of the entire forest, and this led to a form of management called pollarding. Pollarding produces a regular crop of wood like coppicing but, rather than cut right down, trees are cut above head height out of reach of the animals, producing mop-headed trees that can survive to a great age. This creates a landscape known as *wood pasture* – open grazing land with scattered massive trees.

Cattle as well as deer grazed forest areas and the animals were not always fenced out of the woods, in which case the entire wood was pollarded, as can be seen in parts of Epping Forest.

Hatfield Forest is the nearest thing we have to a mediæval forest, with areas of wood-pasture interspersed with patches of coppice woodland, and with deer wandering around. There is nowhere quite like it elsewhere in Britain, let alone in Essex.

Barn Hoppit, Epping Forest
Jeremy Dagley

Forests

Aerial view of Hatfield Forest *a compartmented forest with open, grazed areas – known as 'the plains' – separated (formerly by fences) from the surrounding coppice woods*
David Corke

Epping Forest Act
In the 19th century all the Essex forests came under the threat of enclosure for agriculture or housing. In 1851 most of Hainault Forest was grubbed up, creating a public scandal, and a campaign was mounted to save the neighbouring Epping Forest from a similar fate. This led to the Epping Forest Act of 1878, which appointed the Corporation of London as Conservators of the Forest.

Repairing early damage
The Act placed emphasis on maintaining the 'natural aspect' of Forest – in other words it was not to be turned into a public park. Sadly, this was interpreted as meaning 'leave it to nature'. Without continued cutting of pollard and coppice trees the canopy closed in and the woodland floor lost most of its wild flowers and became dark and bare. Primroses, wood anemones and bluebells used to be widespread but are now few and far between.

A great deal of work has been done since to repair this unintended damage and Epping Forest is as unique in its own way as Hatfield Forest, and remains a magical place to visit.

There are also remnants of mediæval forests in Hainault Forest and Writtle Forest, the latter in private ownership.

Community Forests
A modern attempt has been made to recreate something of the atmosphere of forests in the government's Community Forest initiative of 1990, with sustainable communities as the main objective rather than hunting and venison.

The Thames Chase Community Forest covers parts of east London, Brentwood and Thurrock, and is now approaching 30 years old. Its headquarters near Upminster is included here and other sites within the community forest are covered in other sections, notably in *Grasslands and heaths* (*Tylers Common* on p.56) and in *Rivers and wetlands* (*Ingrebourne Valley* on p.135).

Heathland restoration in Epping Forest
Jeremy Dagley

Epping Forest

Epping Forest covers more than 6,000 acres of land, the main part running in a crescent about 12 miles long from Wanstead in the south to Epping in the north. Although some of the original wildlife diversity of the Forest has been lost, it is still a wonderful place with much to see and enjoy. The many ancient pollard trees are its most striking feature, and especially the great beeches on the higher ground in the central parts.

Epping Forest is set on a ridge of high land between the river valleys of the Lea and Roding, with its highest point a mile or so south of Epping. The ridge consists of patches of gravel laid down by the Thames aeons ago on top of beds of sandy clay, and has a network of springs and water courses.

Probably declared a Forest by Henry I, it was originally part of Waltham Forest, a much larger area, although the wooded area has probably never been much larger than it is now. As Forest Law – the regulations that protected the deer for hunting – declined so parts of it were enclosed and by 1850 no more than 2,000 acres remained.

About one-sixth of Epping Forest was originally open country, and kept so by grazing by deer and cattle. As grazing declined during the 1970s and 1980s, scrub and then trees moved in, and as a result wildlife was lost that requires open, grazed habitats.

Attempts have been under way for some time to reverse the damage and are beginning to show real success, but the road back is slow and difficult after so many years of neglect. Very old pollards, for example, can easily die when repollarded, and birch trees are very difficult to eradicate from former heathland once established.

For all that, Epping Forest remains an unmissable experience. Here we cover the best sections of the Forest, starting with the Lower Forest to the north and working southwards down to Leyton Flats in the heart of east London.

With the overview maps that follow are some brief notes on other parts of the Forest that are also worth a visit.

Epping Forest overview maps

Buffer Lands

One of the aims of the Corporation of London is to protect the 'natural aspect' and the integrity of Epping Forest by acquiring neighbouring land. These 'buffer lands', shown shaded yellow on the maps, consist of a mixture of farmland and woodland. The farmland is used to grow crops or raise livestock and the woodland to produce timber, but in such a way as to benefit wildlife and enhance the local landscape. Public access to some of the buffer lands is possible via footpaths – the main ones are shown on the maps.

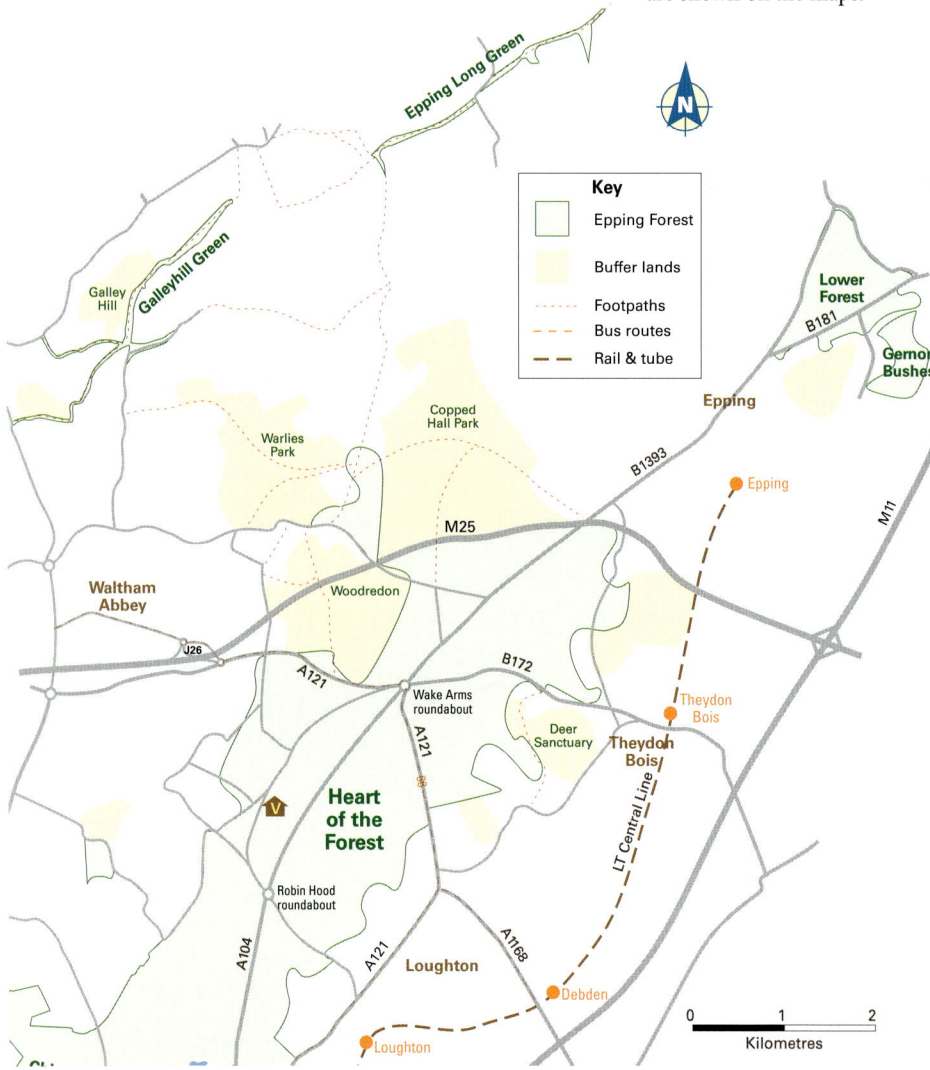

Forests   63

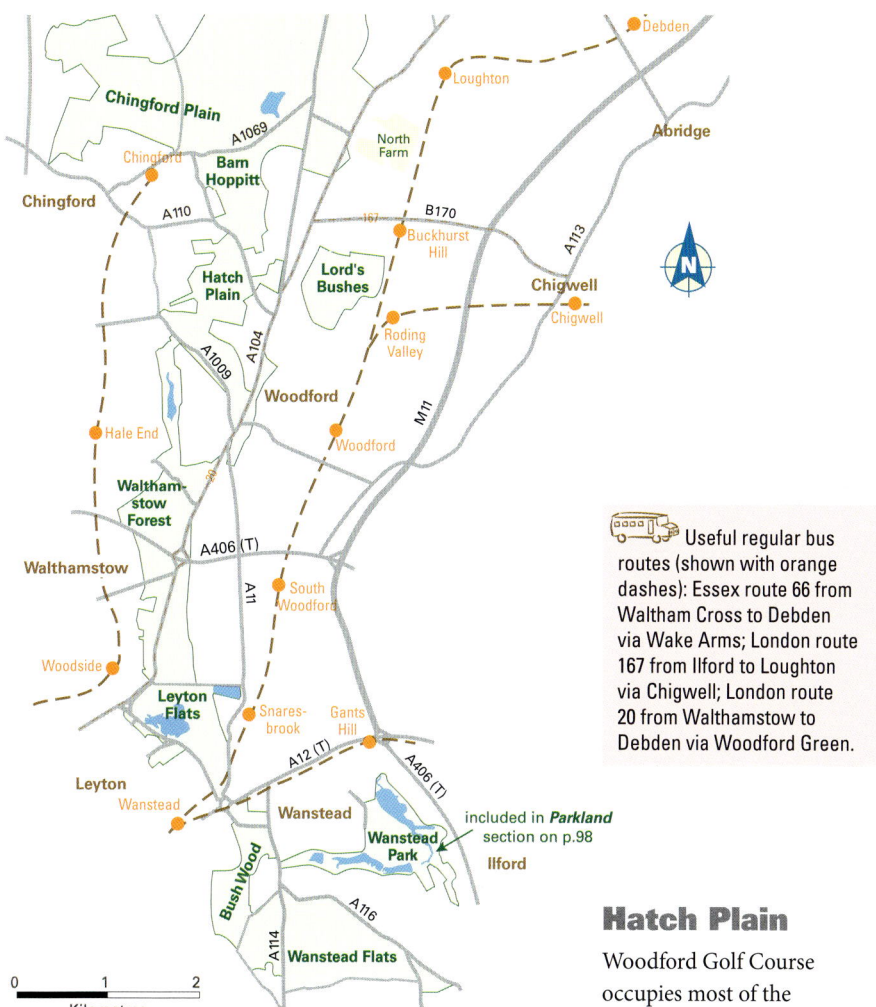

Useful regular bus routes (shown with orange dashes): Essex route 66 from Waltham Cross to Debden via Wake Arms; London route 167 from Ilford to Loughton via Chigwell; London route 20 from Walthamstow to Debden via Woodford Green.

Green Lanes

Galleyhill Green and Epping Long Green are now completely separated from the rest of the Forest, running in an arc starting near Fishers Green in the River Lee Country Park and finishing north of Epping.

They consist of pleasant green lanes interspersed with grassy areas, small woods and occasional ponds. Surrounded as they are by intensive farmland their wildlife value is high. Yellowhammers and linnets, for example, are still seen along them regularly in summer but are now very scarce elsewhere.

Hatch Plain

Woodford Golf Course occupies most of the southern part, surrounded by some attractive grassland with petty whin and heath bedstraw, plus some patches of scrub and many anthills.

Much of the rest is hornbeam woodland, with the River Ching flowing into it from the north. Wood anemones, goldilocks and violets grow on its banks along with some gnarled old hornbeam pollards.

Epping Forest Lower Forest

478ac/191ha   CM16 6TT   TL 475 035   SSSI

The Lower Forest north of Epping is predominantly wood-pasture of oak and hornbeam, much of it dense with holly and scrub. Two broad Green Lanes, bordered by a number of repollarded hornbeams, divide it into four. One of these – Stump Road, once the main road from London to Cambridge – runs alongside Cripsey Brook which has many flowers on its margins, including primroses, dog's mercury, sanicle and angelica. It runs into Wintry Wood Common which is also flower-rich.

Epping Plain at its south-west corner was once open grassland that has been heavily invaded by oak. It has several large ponds with unusual aquatic plants such as water violet and large numbers of dragonflies.

Stump Road

Between High Rd (B1393) and Epping Road (B181) north-east of Epping. There is a parking area on The Woodyard south of the B181.

Buses between Epping and Harlow run along the B1393.

Accessible at all times.

Spring and summer for woodland flowers and insects.

Gernon Bushes

79ac/32ha   CM16 7RN   TL 478 030   SSSI

This is the last remnant of the old Coopersale Common that once linked the Lower Forest to Ongar Park. It has many ancient hornbeam pollards plus some more recent woodland and a network of ponds originally dug for gravel extraction. It descends steeply from the plateau of the ridge across gravelly deposits to London clay lower down.

The gravel workings in the north have developed into sphagnum bogs. In the south two springs rise on the edge of the plateau and their streams descend steep-sided valleys through a series of bogs with large patches of the rare marsh fern. Other notable plants include lady fern, bogbean, marsh valerian, marsh marigold and ragged robin.

Turn off the B181 towards Coopersale village and turn left on to Garnon Mead 200 yards after passing under the railway bridge.

Buses run to Coopersale from Harlow via Epping.

Accessible at all times

Spring for songbirds; summer for marsh plants.

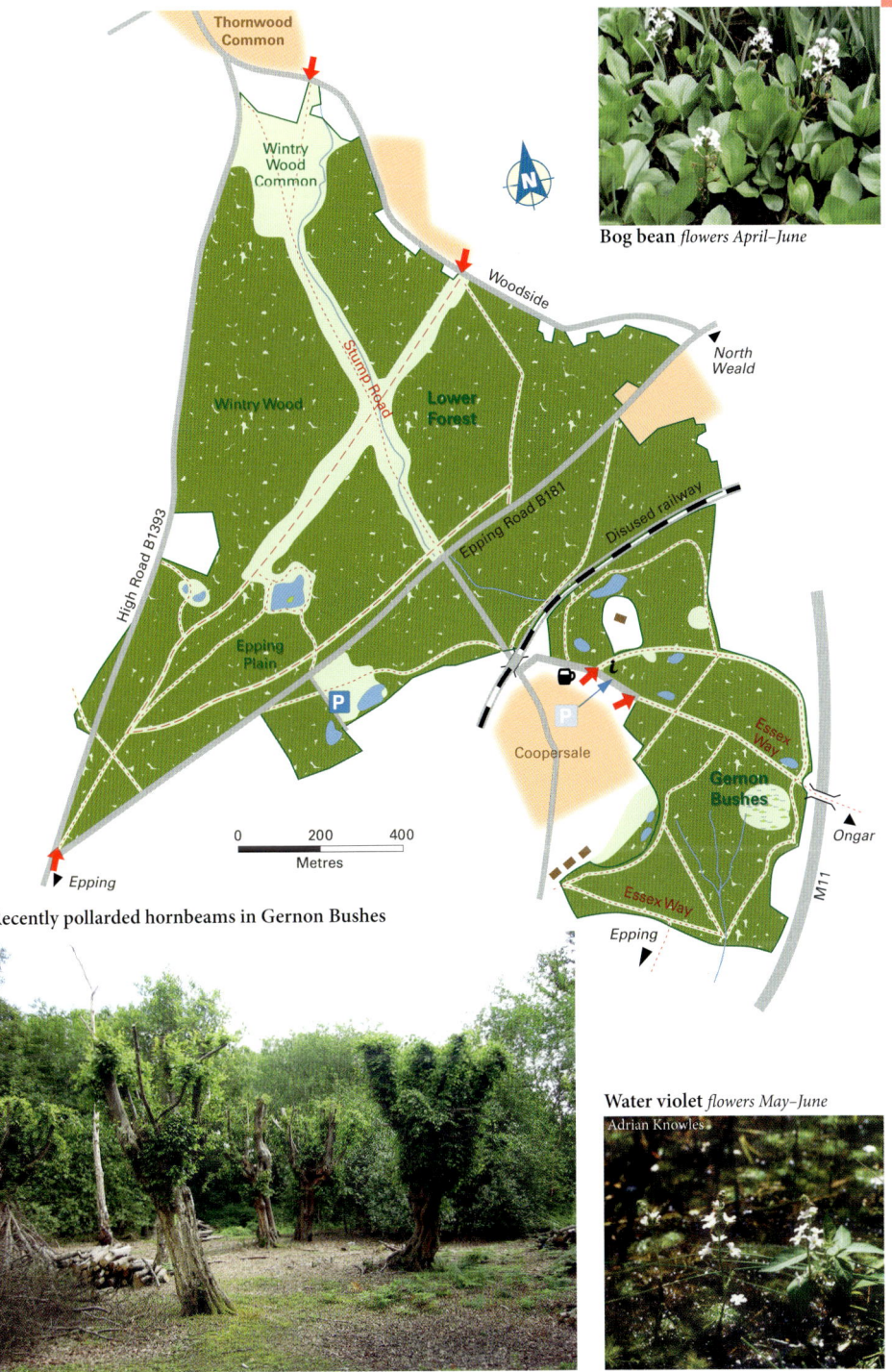

Epping Forest Heart of the Forest

2224ac/900ha   IG10 4AF   TL 412 981   SSSI

The heart of Epping Forest lies to the west of the Epping Forest Conservation Centre at High Beach.

Loughton Camp

Loughton Camp is a circular earth bank believed to date from the late Iron Age. It is set in a woodland of tall beech pollards, with occasional clumps of heather. Below it is Debden Slade, a grassy glade beside a stream with pollard oaks and hornbeams. Many streams run through this area, some with boggy flushes full of ferns, sedges and wetland flowers.

Wake Valley

Wake Valley is a mosaic of beechwood and heathland and has a number of ponds with good dragonfly populations, and especially Wake Valley Pond, in which the downy emerald breeds. The marsh to the north has a good range of wetland plants including ragged robin, lesser spearwort, marsh violet and marsh fern.

Honey Lane Quarters

Honey Lane Quarters slopes down steeply to the west with good views over the Lea Valley. It is wood pasture, with beech at the top and hornbeam lower down. A broad ride leads down to the grassy plain and stream at its foot.

Forests

St Thomas' Quarters

This is mostly beech wood-pasture, with some very large beech pollards. It has a number of streams with boggy flushes and two fine valley bogs east of Lodge Road. Visitor pressure is relatively low so it serves as a refuge for fallow deer.

Long Running

Long Running has the best areas of restored heathland in the Forest. One section is being grazed by cattle and others have been cleared of invading birch. As a result, the original vegetation of cross-leaved heath and ling has reappeared. In the open areas there is a good chance of seeing tree pipits.

Gt & Lt Monk Woods

Here you will find many very old beech and oak pollards, a good number of which have died, creating small clearings in which dense stands of young trees spring up. A number of streams cut deeply into the gravelly slopes.

Furze Ground & Copley Plain

These are restored heathland, surrounded by ancient pollards and some 'coppards', that is trees that have first been coppiced then the multiple stems have been pollarded. The clearings are covered with heather, bracken and purple moorgrass, with occasional boggy areas full of rushes and ferns.

Loughton Brook

Loughton Brook meanders in a deep valley cut through beech and hornbeam wood-pasture, bordered by ferns, sedges, flag iris and heather. Kingfishers and grey wagtails nest along its banks. It leaves the Forest at Staples Pond which has marsh marigolds and a good range of dragonflies.

Leave the M25 at junction 26 and head east along the A121 towards Loughton. A turning on the right just before the roundabout leads to the Conservation Centre.

A long walk from Loughton or Theydon Bois stations on the Central Line, and bus services run from Debden station on the same line.

Forest accessible at all times. Visitor centre open every day except Christmas Day, 11am–6pm summer, 10am–3pm winter.

Worth a visit at any time of year.

Please keep dogs under control at all times and especially near horses. Please keep dogs on leads near livestock.

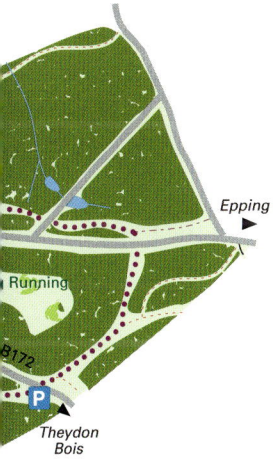

Epping Forest around Chingford

741ac/300ha   E4 7QH   TQ 397 948   SSSI

Much of this area formed the forest's 'plains' – open, grazed areas – and parts of it are grazed by cattle today. Grazing keeps out invading scrub and trees, and encourages low-growing wild flowers such as birdsfoot trefoil, and these in turn attract butterflies and other insects.

The area is also good for birds, because of the variety of habitats, ranging from mature woodland via scrub to open grassland.

The Plains

Whitehouse Plain and Fairmead Bottom are interconnected areas of grassland, some of it damp. Dotted with large patches of scrub and crossed by flower-lined ditches, they are good territory for insects and small mammals. The best of a scattering of ponds is Fairmead Pond, where grass snakes are common.

Much of Chingford Plain is golf course and the rest is open grassland with scattered trees and scrub.

Grass snake

Birdsfoot trefoil *fl. May–August*

Yardley Hill

Once open farmland, Yardley Hill is now virtually covered with oak and thorn scrub. It has patches of chalky soil where plants such as clematis and sweet violet grow. From the top there are good views across the Lea Valley reservoirs into north London. At its foot is Yate's Meadow, which is full of wild flowers in summer and where skylarks and meadow pipits nest.

Leave the M25 at junction 26 and head east along the A121. At the Wake Arms roundabout head south down the A104 and turn right on to the A1069.

Chingford station (Liverpool St line) is a short walk from Queen Elizabeth's Hunting Lodge.

Accessible at all times.

May to early June for breeding birds; summer for wild flowers and insects. To miss the crowds, come in the very early morning and avoid sunny weekends.

Please keep dogs under control at all times and especially near horses, and on leads near livestock.

Many paths are very boggy in winter, and some all year round.

Longhorn grazing on Chingford Plain
Trevor Harris

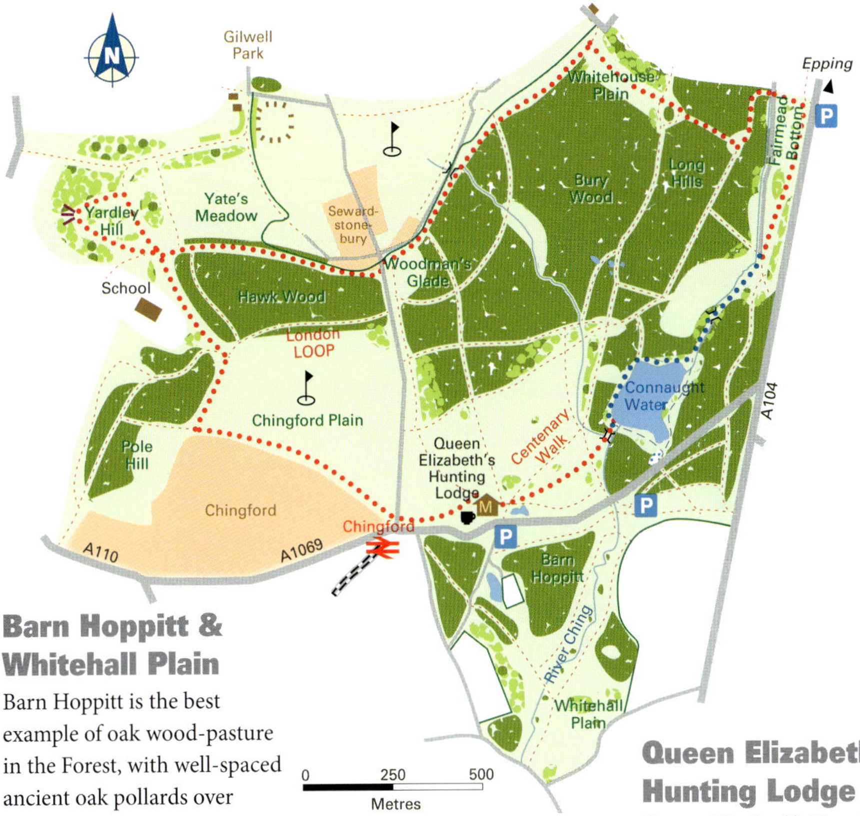

Forests

Barn Hoppitt & Whitehall Plain

Barn Hoppitt is the best example of oak wood-pasture in the Forest, with well-spaced ancient oak pollards over sparse grassland with many anthills and patches of scrub.

The River Ching meanders through from north to south and unusual shrubs such as spindle, alder buckthorn and purple osier grow beside it.

Whitehall Plain has been restored to open grassland after scrubbing over, and now it is cut for hay.

Connaught Water

Connaught Water is a large shallow lake with wooded islands. The grass around it is cropped short by canada geese, and mallard and moorhen breed on its wooded islands. In the winter the Forest's considerable population of mandarin ducks roost there.

Queen Elizabeth's Hunting Lodge

Queen Elizabeth's Hunting Lodge is a three-storey timber-framed building, completed in 1543 by Henry VIII. Its purpose was to provide the monarch and court with a good view of the hunt, and hence its upper windows were originally open. Now, it houses the Epping Forest museum.

Connaught Water
Glyn Baker

Mandarin duck *introduced resident*
Alan Williams

Epping Forest Lord's Bushes

133ac/53ha   *IG9 5HH*   *TQ 413 935*   *SSSI (part)*

Lord's Bushes has many veteran oak and hornbeam pollards and many beech trees as well, some showing signs of old age. Among a variety of other tree species, along the eastern boundary is a grove of wild service trees, an indicator of ancient woodland.

Wide pathways cross the wood, fringed by gorse, sheep's sorrel and pendulous sedge.

Formerly a landscaped garden, Knighton Wood has a mixture of trees – mainly oak, hornbeam and beech with a scattering of exotics – and an attractive lake with islands.

North of Woodford, east of High Road Woodford Green (A121).

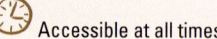 Buckhurst Hill or Roding Valley tube stations are a few minutes' walk.

Accessible at all times.

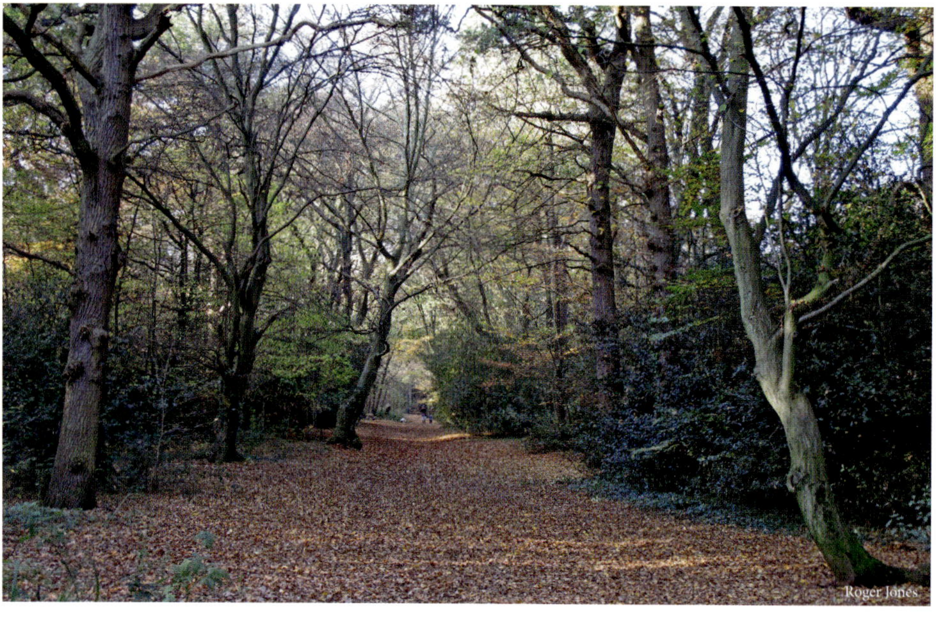

Forests 71

Walthamstow Forest

216ac/86ha   IG8   TQ 391 910   SSSI (part)

Walthamstow Forest was cut in two by the rerouting of the North Circular Road but despite this it still has much to offer. Most of it is wood pasture of oak and hornbeam pollards with a grassy sward beneath in many parts, plus a scattering of ponds and one or two areas of fine open grassland with patches of common cow-wheat and tormentil.

Highams Park to the north is pollard woodland of oak and hornbeam that was landscaped by Humphrey Repton in the 1790s. The River Ching flows into it from the north to feed one of the largest lakes in the Forest, which supports many species of dragonfly. It has carpets of bluebells in spring, along with red campion, wood anemone and periwinkle.

Runs north from the junction between the A406 North Circular and A104 Woodford New Road.

Highams Park station is a short walk away. Buses from Walthamstow and Loughton run along Woodford New Road.

Accessible at all times.

Red campion *flowers April–October*

Tormentil *flowers June–August*

Epping Forest: Gilbert's Slade & Leyton Flats

316ac/126ha **E11 1PQ** **TQ 395 891** **SSSI**

Gilbert's Slade, to the east of Woodford New Road, is open woodland with many fine old gnarled oak and hornbeam pollards and an open glade at its centre. It has many patches of common cow-wheat and tormentil, with heather here and there.

Rising Sun Wood across the road also has many old pollards, principally hornbeam, and because it was grazed until very recently it still has the feel of old wood-pasture. It too has an open glade, Canada Plain, surrounding Bulrush Pond.

Most of Leyton Flats is acid grassland, kept open by cattle grazing. It has large patches of gorse and broom, which are well used by birds for nesting, and is also the London stronghold for creeping willow. The northern section has mature oak woodland and an interesting marshy area of shallow pools and willow scrub. It has two large ponds: Hollow Pond, used for boating, and Eagle Pond. Eagle Pond, one of the oldest in the Forest, is quite deep in places and has a large concentration of mute swans.

East of the Whipps Cross roundabout (A104/A114), running alongside Woodford New Road up to the A406 North Circular Road to the north.

 Snaresbrook tube station is a short walk from Eagle Pond. Buses from Romford to Walthamstow via Ilford run past Hollow Pond.

Accessible at all times.

Mute swan *resident*
Reston Kilgour

Forests

Wanstead Flats

450ac/182ha *E11 3QS* *TQ 407 862* *SSSI (part)*

The former Wanstead Heath has a long history of grazing by local commoners, which saved it from destruction by private landowners in the 18th century. Since then it has been dissected by several main roads and much of it has been resown and levelled for football pitches. The remainder is still grazed by cattle.

It contains some of London's most extensive acid grassland, with small areas of ling heather and petty whin, a low-growing form of gorse. It also supports many unusual insects, including stag beetles, and nesting skylarks.

It has six ponds, but only Alexandra Lake and Jubilee Pond retain water all year.

It also includes Bush Wood, a mature woodland, mainly oak, with some grassy glades and some massive trees, including some very large sweet chestnuts. Its birdlife includes great spotted woodpeckers, tawny owls and long-tailed tits. In the grassland to the south there is an historic avenue of lime trees.

Between Wanstead and Forest Gate, south of Aldersbrook Road.

Train to Wanstead Park or Manor Park; several bus services.

Accessible at all times. Car parks open daylight hours.

Skylark *resident*

Forests

Hainault Forest

What remains of Hainault Forest lies on the north-eastern boundary of Greater London on a miniature version of the ridge that forms Epping Forest – a cap of gravelly and sandy soils over London clay.

Hainault Forest

291ac/118ha   IG7 5PG   TQ 475 938   SSSI

WOODLAND TRUST

After it was 'disafforested' in 1851 most of Hainault Forest was destroyed for housing and farming. The remaining woodland was managed as wood pasture until about 1900, when pollarding stopped as the markets for charcoal and firewood declined.

Now, the Woodland Trust is repollarding some of the old trees and also raising new trees for pollarding. Pollarding rejuvenates trees but after a long gap it is very risky.

To the east is ancient woodland, dominated by hornbeam pollards – some 6,000 in total – and oak standards, with holly, bracken and bramble growing beneath them. Much of the woodland floor is bare because of the dense shade cast by the overgrown pollards, but it has many damp areas and ditches that are greener and more varied, often lined with pendulous sedge. If you look around you will find unusual plants like wood speedwell, hartstongue fern, marsh pennywort and butcher's broom.

To the west the woodland is very different. It has regenerated on sections that were cleared and is dominated by oak and birch with some aspen, poplar and ash.

Off the A1112 a mile south of Chigwell Row. Enter from the south via the A12 (London – Chelmsford) and from the north via the A113 (Woodford – Chelmsford).

The nearest station is Hainault (Central line tube), from where buses run to the main entrance. Buses also run from Romford, Chadwell Heath and Barkingside.

Accessible at all times. The Foxburrows Road car park is open every day from 7.00am to dusk; peripheral car parks on Manor Road are always open.

May/June for songbirds; or try a misty winter day to see the fantastic tree shapes in the ancient woodland.

Butcher's broom
Owen Keen

Pollarding in progress in Hainault Forest

Hainault Forest Country Park

247ac/100ha   IG7 4QW   TQ 475 928

What is now the country park was part of Hainault Forest's 'plains' and therefore was treeless, but it was invaded by birch and scrub when grazing ceased. Now, the dense cover attracts many breeding birds.

The many areas of rough grassland sheltered by trees make good feeding territory for bats, which find roosting sites in the ancient trees. A number of different species can be seen feeding over the lake on warm evenings, including pipistrelles, noctules and daubenton's bats.

Greylag and canada geese, mute swans and mallards nest on and around the lake. They have been joined recently by egyptian geese, an introduced species once restricted to north Norfolk that has been spreading into London's parks.

Egyptian geese *introduced resident*

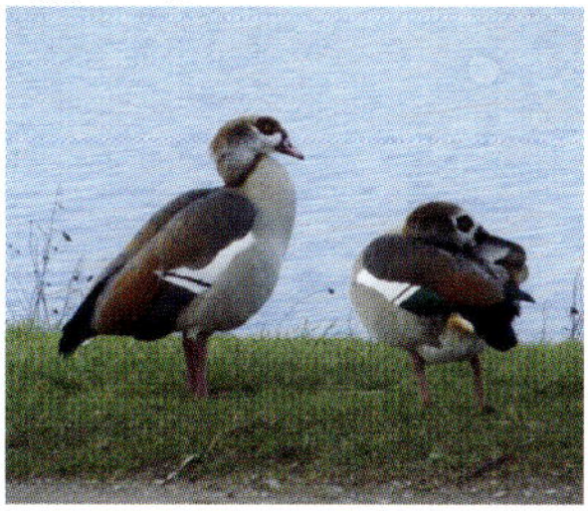

In the north-west corner a small area of former heathland has been restored by removing invading birch and scrub, and heather and dwarf gorse have recolonised.

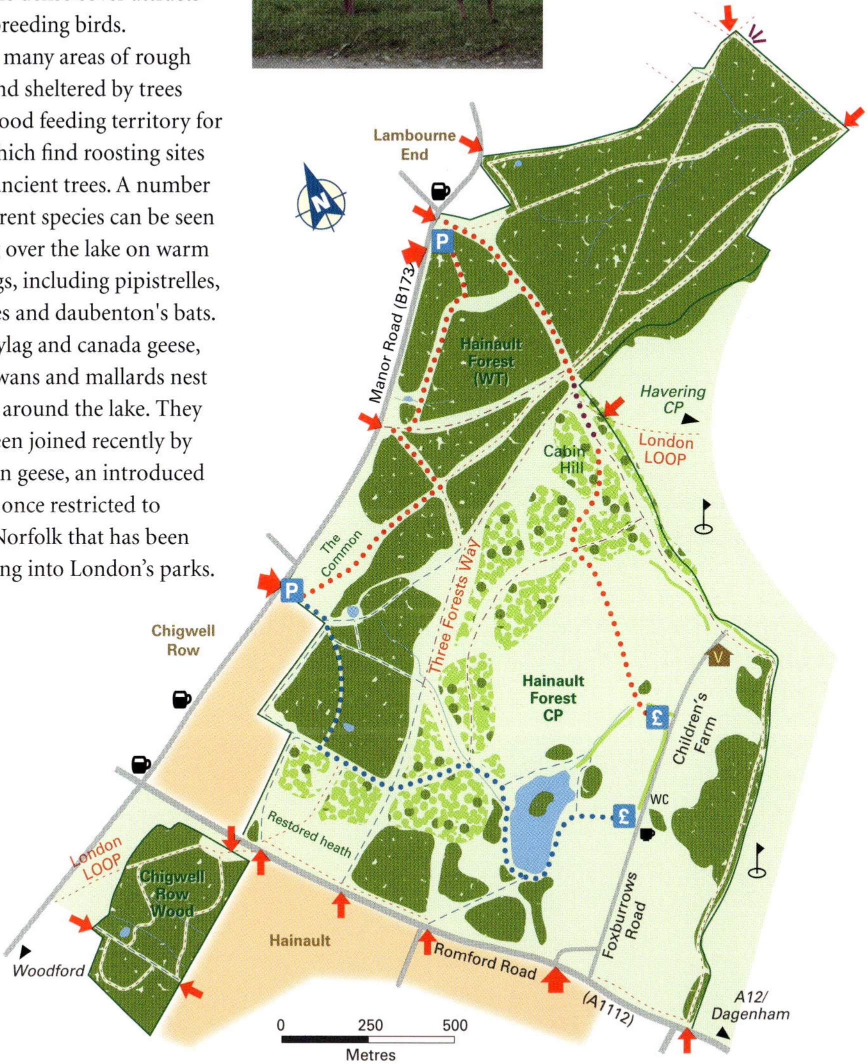

Hatfield Forest

1049ac/420ha   CM22 6LH   TL 547 202   SSSI, NNR

Hatfield Forest is a compartmented forest, with open grazed areas separated from the wooded areas by ditches and banks designed to keep out grazing animals. Trees scattered across the plains are pollarded, in other words cut above head height where grazing animals cannot reach, while the wooded compartments are managed by coppicing.

Ancient pollard trees are what make Hatfield Forest so special. It has about 600 pollards in total, including not only oak and hornbeam, which can be seen elsewhere in Essex, but also many maple and hawthorn, which are rare as pollards, and just a handful of beech, lineage elm and crab apple. Nowhere else can you see such a variety of species and form. It is also the stronghold in Essex of mistletoe, which is widespread on the ancient hawthorns and maples on the plains.

The woods consist mainly of ash, hazel, and an unusually large number of maple. There are also some gigantic coppice stools of oak, particularly in Lodge Coppice to the west, while the west end of Street Coppice has four acres of alder on a plateau – alder is a plant of wet, flushed ground, in other words where water is moving through the soil, picking up oxygen as it goes.

The predominant woodland plant is dog's mercury but the coppice woodlands also support a wide range of other flowers including indicators

Dog's mercury *fl. March–April*

of ancient woodland such as oxlips (mainly in or near Hamptons Coppice) and herb paris (in Long Coppice).

Shermore Brook runs through the Forest from north to south, feeding into a chalky fen above the lake, around which are a number of rare plants, including marsh willowherb and marsh pennywort. Water rail are usually present here also.

Marshy areas around the fen, and another to the north called Old Woman's Weaver, are full of wetland plants and alive with insects in summer.

A range of woodland birds breed in the Forest, including nightingale, plus the odd woodcock and hawfinch. Feeding flocks of hawfinches, redwings and fieldfares can sometimes be seen in winter.

Hatfield Forest in autumn
Glyn Baker

Forests

Turn south off the B1256 (Bishop's Stortford–Takeley) in Takeley Street, about 3 miles east of M11 junction 8. Limited car parking in the winter months.

Buses run to Takeley Street from Bishop's Stortford and Braintree/Dunmow: get off at Green Man PH.

Open dawn to dusk daily. Café open daily 9am–5pm, April to end October, otherwise 9am–3pm.

March to see the golden mistletoe stems on the trees in the plains; May for birdsong and spring flowers; July for butterflies in the open areas and along the rides.

Dogs on leads near livestock and around lake. Dog-free area near lake.

Woodside Green

Alongside Wall Wood lies Woodside Green, an ancient common consisting of open grassland with scattered ancient trees, now grazed by cattle.

Wall Wood

Wall Wood was one of Hatfield Forest's 'purlieu woods', which were associated with the Forest but not entirely part of it.

It has many ancient coppiced trees and, in the more open parts, good ground flora – carpets of dog's mercury, patches of bluebells and a scattering of primroses.

Thames Chase Forest Centre

140ac/56ha   RM14 3NS   TQ 583 862

The former Broadfields Farm is now the Thames Chase Forest Centre, headquarters of the Thames Chase Trust. New woodlands have been planted over much of the site, and its broad rides and occasional glades have been sown with a grass and wildflower mix. There are two ponds, one with a hide and one a dipping platform, and a network of paths, most of them fully accessible.

This is a large site and is developing a great deal of wildlife interest as it matures. Skylarks nest in the open grassland, and birds such as green woodpecker, yellowhammer, willow warbler and whitethroat exploit the young woodland.

It also has a good population of bats, taking advantage of the many batboxes that have been installed.

The section east of the M25 can be reached via an underpass (and is best visited when the wind is from the east, i.e. towards the motorway). It is comparatively undisturbed and has good numbers of nesting birds and small mammals.

Main entrance off Pike Lane, a narrow lane running south from St Mary's Lane (B187) a mile east of Upminster.

Upminster station is about 20 minutes' walk.

Site open 8.30am to dusk. Visitor centre open 10am–5pm (10am–4pm November to late March).

Cycles for hire weekends and school holidays April–Oct.

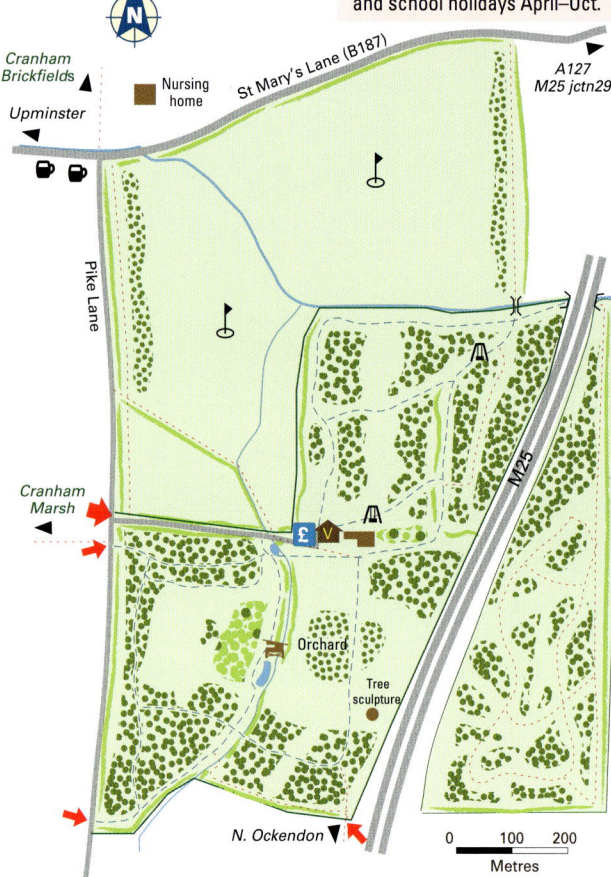

Green woodpecker
Alan Williams

Writtle Forest

500ac/200ha   CM4 0RH   TL 638 012

Sizeable parts of what was once Writtle Forest survive in private ownership but are still accessible via public footpaths and bridleways. These woods have all the diversity and also much of the wildness that you might have found in mediæval woods – areas dense with bracken and bramble and others where the woodland floor is dark and bare; little streams and bogs; occasional glades. The trees are mainly sweet chestnut coppice, with oak and hornbeam in the damper parts, and maple, spindle and dogwood on the fringes.

Unlike Hatfield Forest, Writtle Forest had the woods in the middle and the plains – open areas used for grazing – around the outside. Mill Green Common is a surviving part of the plains. It has been invaded by birch and other trees, but still has some heather in the open parts, which are alive with insects in summer.

North of Ingatestone and west of Chelmsford. Take the minor road from the centre of Ingatestone to Fryerning. Turn right and follow Mill Green Road to Mill Green, or turn left and follow Blackmore Road to reach Fryerning Wood and Maple Tree Lane.

Accessible at all times.

May–June for early flowers and birdsong; July–August for flowers and butterflies.

Many of the paths are used by horses and can be boggy and wet even in the summer.

Writtle Forest (continued)

Maple Tree Lane is a broad ancient green lane, bounded for much of its length by ditches and banks topped with twisted coppice stools of hornbeam and massive oaks. Short sections have been surfaced, but for most of the way the tracks followed by horses (and with more difficulty, people) meander round patches of bramble and scrub and occasional pools and boggy areas.

Parkland
Keeping up with the royals

Parks were introduced to Britain by the Normans. For them parks were deer parks, and the wealthy few who could afford it kept them for venison, a luxury food in those days, and as status symbols. In the 12th century there were approaching 2,000 deer parks in Britain, and mainly in England. By the 17th century most of them had fallen out of use, and parks were increasingly seen as landscape rather than a source of venison.

A few mediæval deer parks have survived as they were, but many were converted by the great park designers of the 18th century, such as Lancelot 'Capability' Brown and Humphry Repton. Some still are private parks but many fell into public ownership as their owners ran short of money and management costs increased, and are now being managed for landscape and amenity, and often for wildlife as well. Probably because their clients wanted instant results and newly planted trees take so long to grow, park designers usually retained some of the original features, such as the ancient pollard trees, the hedgerows and the woods. To this they added the exotic planting, the ornamental features and the good views that the owners wanted.

Combined with sympathetic management, this variety of features leads in turn to a diversity of wildlife.

Parkland

Bedfords Park

215ac/87ha   *RM4 1QH*   *TQ 518 924*

Bedfords Park was enclosed in the 15th century and the manor house and gardens were laid out around it later. The park was acquired by the local council in 1933, but the manor house fell into disrepair and was demolished in 1959. Now it is managed as an urban park.

The upper section has all the scenic grandeur of landscaped parkland, with its exotic trees, its deer enclosure and its close-mown slopes. The lower section is managed for wildlife, with hay meadows and some mature woodland and scrub.

The area of marsh to the east of the north–south bridleway is fed by springs seeping out at the top of the slope. Beyond it is a large meadow which is one of the finest flower-rich grasslands in Essex. Here you will find cuckoo flower, pignut and ragged robin flowering in spring, and later knapweed, sneezewort and pepper saxifrage.

Birdlife is varied with many warbler species arriving in summer to breed, particularly in the scrub and woodland in the south of the park. A wide variety of dragon- and damselflies can be seen around the lake and ponds in summer.

Parks were often sited to get the best views, and this one is no exception. From the visitor centre, sited near the now-demolished Bedfords House and run by Essex Wildlife Trust, there are superb views across Essex and into Kent.

 Between Harold Hill and Havering-atte-Bower, former site of a royal palace. The main entrance is off Broxhill Road, which runs north from Lower Bedfords Road up to Havering-atte-Bower village.

 Frequent bus services run from Romford station (Liverpool St line) to the bottom end of the park on Lower Bedfords Road. Occasional services run to Havering-atte-Bower past the main entrance.

 Centre open daily 9am to 5pm (4pm in winter) exc. Xmas and Boxing Day. Vehicle entrance closes at dusk.

 May–June for wild flowers and birdsong, and July to September for later flowers and flying insects.

Sneezewort flowers July–August
Owen Keen

The bridleway in Bedfords Park
Roger John

Parkland 83

Red deer in the Bedfords Park enclosure

Belhus Belhus Woods Country Park

180ac/72ha   *RM15 4XJ*   *TQ 565 825*

Essex County Council

The Belhus estate dates from the 14th century. Originally a deer park, it was landscaped by Capability Brown in the 18th century.

The main part, east of Romford Road, has ancient woodland, grassland, and five lakes that were created by gravel extraction. Two of these are used for fishing and the others are reserved for wildlife. the clearings are full of wild flowers in summer, including (as it is a damp wood) marsh thistles and ragged robin. West of Romford Road are two ancient woods, surrounded by the Forestry Commission's plantings of Cely Woods (see opposite). Warwick Wood is especially interesting, with aspen groves and many surviving elm trees.

On Romford Road between Upminster and Aveley, reached from the south via the A13/A1306 and B1335.

Half-hourly service from Romford to Lakeside via Upminster station runs along Romford Road.

Belhus Woods main entrance open 8am–dusk, and visitor centre 9am–4pm. Access via public footpaths at all times.

May–July for birdsong, butterflies and dragonflies. Choose a day with a westerly wind to reduce the noise from the M25 nearby.

Mobility scooters available from the centre.

With such a variety of habitats the park is rich in wildlife, including a wide variety of flowering plants. Brick Kiln Wood with its streams and ponds, dug to extract clay for brickmaking, is alive with insects in summer, as are the meadows nearby.

The hazel in Running Water Wood is being coppiced and

Parkland

Belhus Woods lake

Marsh thistle *fl. July–August*

Cely Woods

141ac/57ha *RM13 9EW* *TQ 560 828*

Cely Woods is former farmland surrounding the ancient woodlands of Warwick and White Post Woods, part of it planted up with mainly native broad-leaved trees. Open meadows have been left between the plantings and support many wild flowers.

Natural regeneration from the ancient woods has been encouraged and here some valuable habitat has developed. Many flying insects are attracted in summer, including small heath butterflies.

Running Water Brook crosses the site and an attractive small wetland has been created nearby.

Belhus Chase

134ac/54ha *RM15 4XH* *TQ 567 822*

This land to the south of Belhus Woods Country Park was acquired by the Woodland Trust in 1998 as part of its *Woods on your Doorstep* project. Part has been planted with trees – now maturing – and part left as open meadows, to create a parkland atmosphere.

Claybury Park

177ac/71.5ha   IG5 0XH   TQ 435 911   SSSI (part)

Claybury Park occupies the south-facing slopes of a ridge east of Woodford Bridge. It includes parkland associated with Claybury Hall and ancient woodland formerly in the grounds of Claybury Hospital. From high on the slope there are spectacular views over East London, Docklands and the Kent hills.

The parkland design was influenced by Humphry Repton, who lived not far away in Romford. Several historic landscape features have survived, including Cocked Hat Plantation (a linear woodland of oak, birch and hornbeam), Ash Plantation (dense elm scrub with mature oak and grey poplar – no ash!) and Egg Clump (oak, ash and hawthorn).

The western part of the ancient woodland, Claybury Wood, contains many ancient hornbeam coppice stools and pollard oaks and is carpeted with bluebells and wood anemones in spring. It also has many wild service trees, butcher's broom and broad-leaved helleborine orchids. Hospital Hill Wood to the east is a fine woodland dominated by oak.

The soils are varied and this makes for variety in the grassland plants. These support a variety of the commoner grassland butterflies, including small heath.

Just east of Woodford Bridge. Follow Fulwell Avenue west from the Fulwell Cross roundabout (A123), or leave the M11/North Circular Road (A406) at their junction and follow Southend Road (A1400) east, turning left into Roding Lane North. On-street parking.

Fairlop tube station (Central line) is on Forest Road about 100m east of Fulwell Cross. Or train to Ilford then bus 169.

Open daylight hours only.

Something of interest at all times of the year, but especially May for songbirds and July/August for grassland butterflies and other insects.

A good network of surfaced paths.

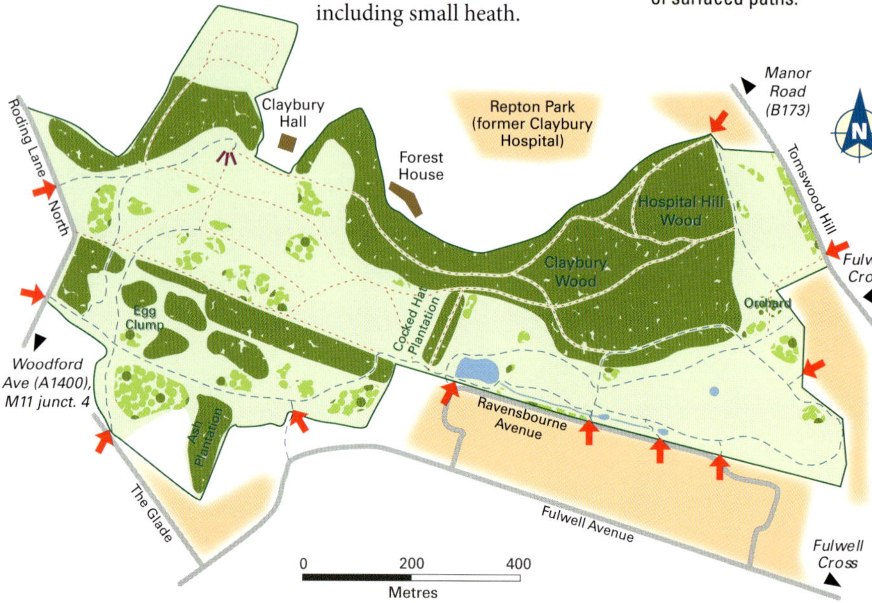

Parkland 87

Fordham Hall Estate

500ac/205ha   CO6 3LY   TL 926 277

WOODLAND TRUST

This is a former arable farm surrounding the village of Fordham. More than 47,000 trees have been planted to create 300 acres of new woodland. Some 15km of hedgerows, some probably ancient in origin, have been retained.

Most of the remaining 200 acres adjoining the River Colne have been resown with grass and wild flowers and are being managed by cutting for hay and grazing by sheep and cattle.

The River Colne runs along the southern boundary within steep banks and the meadows alongside are marshy and flood in winter. The dampest patches support wetland species such as purple loosestrife, brooklime and yellow iris. Mature willows and alders grow along the river bank.

The wildlife potential of such a large area is considerable and many bird and bat boxes have been put up to encourage colonisation. Otters and water voles occupy the river, barn owls are seen regularly and skylarks nest in the open fields.

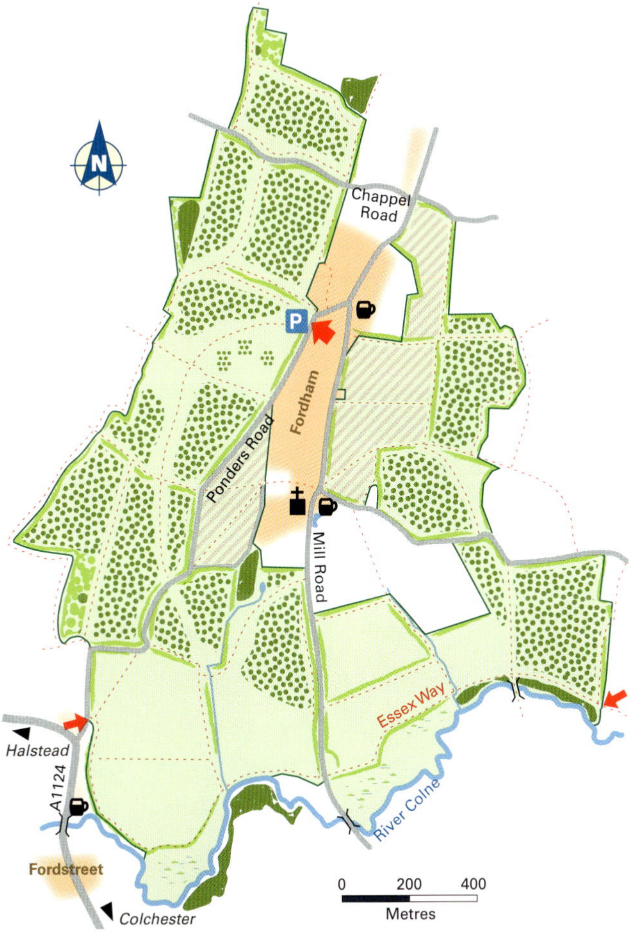

Turn off the A1124 (Colchester–Halstead) in the village of Fordstreet, on to Ponders Road. There is a parking area on the left shortly after you reach Fordham village.

Hourly bus service Colchester–Halstead runs through Fordstreet.

Accessible at all times.

Spring for breeding birds; summer for flying insects and wild flowers in the meadows; warm summer evenings for bats.

Brooklime *flowers May–September*

Parkland

Havering Country Park

150ac/60ha   RM5 3PH   TQ 500 924

This was once part of the estate of Havering Palace. One of the historic features that has survived is an avenue of wellingtonia trees (also known as giant redwoods) along Wellingtonia Avenue in the north-east corner.

The park is mainly mature mixed woodland, including some ancient hazel coppice and one of the few established pine woodlands in the area, which attracts pine specialists such as goldcrests (which breed here) and coal tits.

High on the ridge the soil is gravelly and here you find birch, gorse and bracken, while the damper, heavier clay soil of the southern valley favours oak, hornbeam and bramble.

The wildflower meadows to the south are cut for hay in September. Agrimony, birdsfoot trefoil and ox-eye daisies grow here.

Ox-eye daisies *flower June–July*

Access via Clockhouse Lane, which runs north from the roundabout in Collier Row where Collier Row Lane (B174) meets Chase Cross Road.

Frequent buses run from Romford and terminate at the main entrance.

Accessible at all times. Car parks open from dawn to dusk.

May for songbirds and early flowers in the woodland; June–July for wild flowers in the meadows; autumn for tree colours.

Vehicle access to easy access trail from Wellingtonia Avenue via a radar key obtainable from Havering Council or from the Park Office (01708 720858).

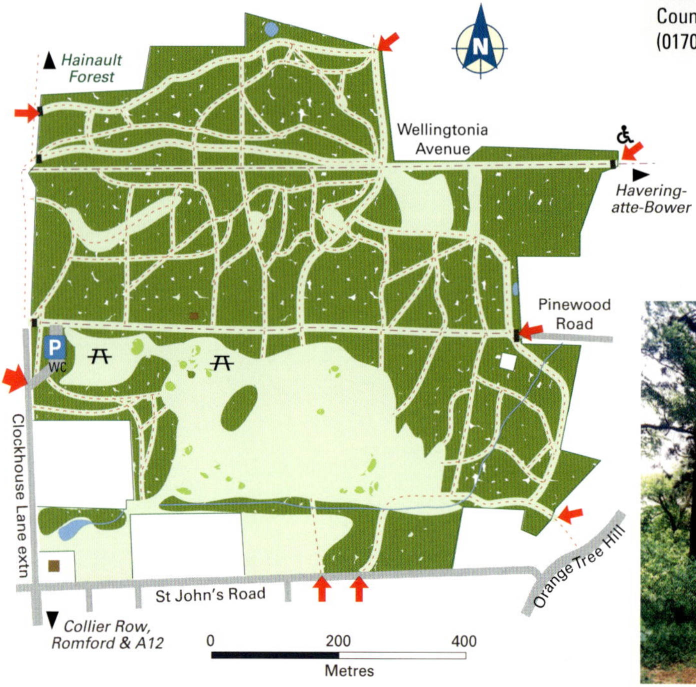

Wellingtonia Avenue
Alan Cooper

Parkland   89

High Woods Country Park

330ac/132ha   CO4 5JR   TL 998 271

Colchester

High Woods Country Park occupies land that was once part of the Royal Forest of Kingswood. Today it is a patchwork of woods, meadows, marsh and rough ground.

The woods in the stream valley to the north, known as the Central Valley, are a remnant of Kingswood Forest and are being coppiced. The valley floor is mainly ash and alder, with small-leaved lime and oak on the slopes. In April it is carpeted with bluebells.

The mosaic of trees, scrub and open grassland in the eastern section suits a variety of nesting birds, including willow warblers, whitethroats and goldfinches. In autumn it is full of berries and wild fruit.

Friars Grove is a small ancient valley wood, surrounded by its original earth bank and ditch.

A large area of marshland has developed around the stream before it passes under the railway and this provides cover for birds such as sedge warblers and reed buntings. In summer the many insects overhead attract crowds of swifts, swallows and martins and, on warm nights, bats.

Main entrance off Turner Road, which leaves the A134 Colchester–Sudbury road north of Colchester North station.

Footpath from the station enters just south of the railway bridge over the A134.

Car parks open 7.30 am–10 pm in summer, 7pm in winter. Visitor centre open daily April–September, otherwise weekends only, 10 am–4 pm.

April for bluebells; May/June for breeding birds in woodland and scrub; summer for wild flowers and flying insects.

Cycle route from Castle Park enters from the south.

Marshy meadow in High Woods
Glyn Baker

Parkland

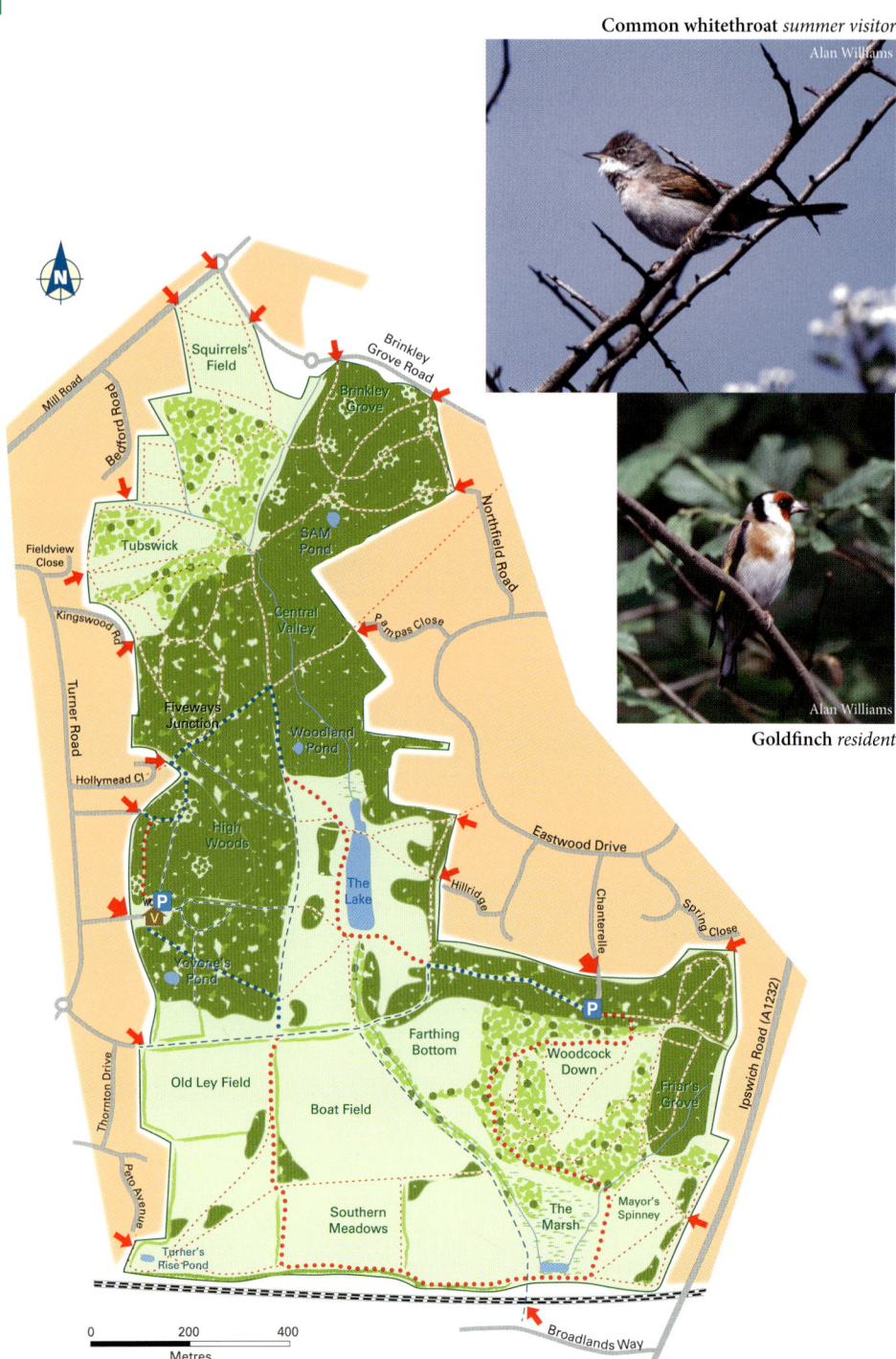

Common whitethroat *summer visitor*
Alan Williams

Goldfinch *resident*
Alan Williams

Parkland 91

Hylands Park

578ac/234ha   CM2 8FS   TL 683 043

Many people will associate Hylands Park with events such as the annual V-Festival, but in fact it is an historic park offering a great deal for anyone interested in wildlife. Landscaped parkland, designed by Humphry Repton in the 18th century, surrounds Hylands House and its formal garden. Later the estate was extended from its original 213 acres to nearly 600 today.

As you would expect of a long-established wood-pasture, it has some fine ancient trees, and also some patches of ancient woodland. The largest of these, South Wood, is former coppice rich in flowers, including large numbers of early purple orchids.

Add to this some flower-rich grassland, a number of ponds – with a thriving population of great crested newts – and a stretch of the River Wid. A herd of fallow deer graze within the park but are not enclosed within it.

Access from the A414 about a mile west of the St Mary's Church roundabout, at the southern end of Chelmsford's inner ring road. Signed cycle route from Writtle village.

Bus 351 Brentwood to Chelmsford: from Chelmsford nearest bus stop is next to the St Mary's Church roundabout; from Brentwood on London Road outside the entrance gates.

Gates open at 7.30am and close at dusk. Stables Centre open daily, excluding Christmas and Boxing Day. Sometimes access may be restricted because of events.

Late April to May for early purple orchids in South Wood.

South Wood

Marks Hall Estate

450ac/180ha   CO6 1TG   TL 841 255

Marks Hall Estate is an ancient estate set in attractive countryside north of Coggeshall. It runs to some 2,000 acres, of which 150 are enclosed and hold an arboretum and formal gardens and a further 300 acres are accessible via footpaths. The estate was left to the nation by its last owner, Thomas Phillips Price.

Great wildlife interest can be found in the old deer park – which sadly has lost nearly all of its massive ancient oaks – and in a large area of ancient woodland. Some of these woods have been planted with conifers but a great amount of the original woodland remains, containing a number of wild service trees and large areas of small-leaved lime, a tree that once dominated the woods of East Anglia but now confined to just a few ancient woods.

The woods are being coppiced and this encourages flowering plants such as lily of the valley, sweet woodruff and early purple orchid. They are frequented by deer and a wide range of woodland birds, including nightingales. Rare breed pigs are held in movable enclosures in the woods and perform the same function as wild boars used to, turning over the soil looking for food. Highland cattle graze the open grassland.

With its grassy tracks, coppiced woods and ancient hedgerows, Marks Hall is especially good for butterflies, including silver-washed fritillaries.

Small-leaved lime

Pat Allen

Reached via a turning off the B1024 to Earls Colne north of Coggeshall: follow the brown-and-white signs from the A120.

The Visitor Centre – housed in a 15th-century barn – is normally open from Easter until 31st October except non-Bank Holiday Mondays,10.30am to 5pm, otherwise Fridays and weekends only, 10.30am to 4.30pm. Admission £5.50 adults, £2.50 children 5 and over. Accessible via public footpaths at all times, but permissive paths and the gardens are only open during visitor centre hours.

Spring for woodland flowers and birdsong; summer for butterflies.

Parkland 93

The Manor

174ac/70ha   RM3 9XR   TQ 551 928   LNR

Dagnam Park, which forms most of The Manor LNR, was part of the former Manor of Dagnam. Across the centre is ancient parkland, sandwiched between two small ancient woods. The ancient grasslands extending to the east towards Fir Wood are managed as hay meadows, and are rich in wild flowers and insects in summer.

The many large patches of scrub and the ancient trees serve as nest sites for a variety of birds. Hawfinches often visit in winter. It has a number of ponds in most of which great crested newts breed.

Former farmland to the north and west of the original park was added in 2015. Surrounded by mature hedgerows, these fields are relatively undisturbed and large herds of fallow deer gather here.

Fallow deer in The Manor

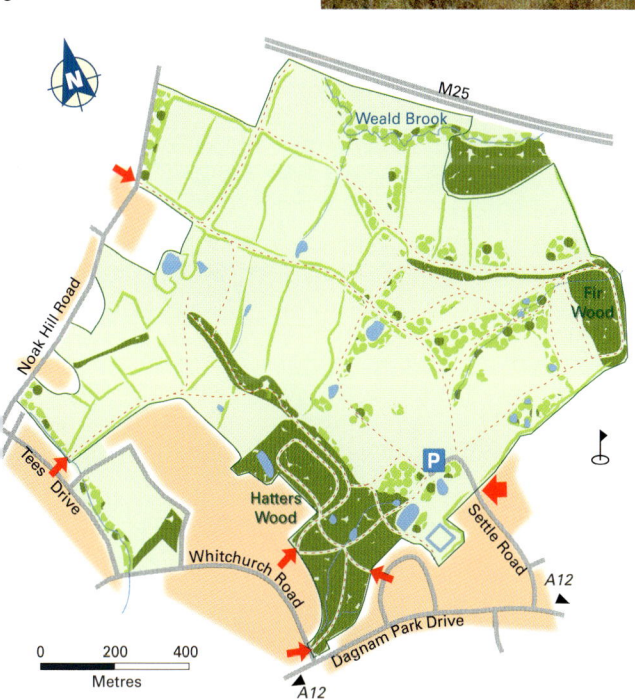

Off Settle Road in the north of Harold Hill. Turn off the A12 on to Gooshays Drive east of Gallows Corner, then turn right at the roundabout on to Dagnam Park Drive. Settle Road turns off on the left.

Bus services from Romford run along Dagnam Park Drive.

Accessible at all times.

May to August for birds, wild flowers and insects.

Parkland

Thorndon

Essex County Council's Thorndon Country Park is right next to The Old Park, which is former farmland planted up by the Woodland Trust. These make up a very large area of public access land with a network of paths and a variety of habitats, including ancient woodland, former wood-pasture, recent broad-leaved and older conifer plantations, ponds, marsh, recovering heath and cattle-grazed pasture.

Thorndon Country Park

529ac/214ha   CM13 3RZ   TQ 605 915   SSSI (part)

Essex County Council

The area now occupied by Thorndon Country Park first became a deer park in the 15th century, but its present shape was established in the 18th when it was landscaped by Capability Brown for the owner, Lord Petre of Thorndon Hall. It became a country park in the 1950s.

Originally it was in two separate parts, the northern section on a gravel ridge and the southern part on clay soil lower down. These are now connected via a block of small hedged fields known as Old Thorndon Pastures, grazed by British White rare breed cattle.

Ancient trees are a special feature, scattered throughout the woods and also in the former wood-pasture, now called The Deer Park. Notably, there are huge beech trees near the centre in Thorndon North, and some giant former pollard oaks and hornbeams.

Parts of the park used to be heathland, now a scarce habitat, and to restore it sections are being grazed on rotation by goats and sheep.

It has two large ponds: Childerditch Pond in Thorndon North, with a small marsh and an open meadow to its north, and Old Hall Pond in Thorndon South.

The park attracts a wide variety of birds, and sometimes spectacular numbers of winter visitors such as siskins, redpolls and bramblings. It supports many butterflies, including the white-letter hairstreak.

Brambling *male, winter visitor*

Crinoline Oak in The Deer Park

The Old Park

135ac/54ha   CM13 3RZ   TQ 620 906

WOODLAND TRUST

Hatch Farm separated the two parts of the original Thorndon Country Park. It was built as a 'model farm' in the 18th century to raise deer and cattle.

A large part of it has been acquired by the Woodland Trust as one of its Plant-a-Wood sites. Oak, ash, sweet chestnut and hornbeam have been planted in blocks and the remainder sown with grass and wildflower seed, to create a parkland atmosphere.

It also includes a small patch of (possibly ancient) woodland called *The Rookery*, which surrounds an attractive small pond.

Parkland

South of Brentwood and west of the A128 (Ongar–Brentwood–A127). The main entrance to Thorndon North is off The Avenue, which links the A128 and the B186 (Brentwood–South Ockendon). The entrance to Thorndon South is off the A128 just north of its junction with the A127.

Brentwood station is about 2km (via Hartswood and Little Warley Common) from Thorndon North.

Open all year from 8am to dusk. The visitor centre in Thorndon North is open every day from 9am to 5pm (4pm in winter).

May for spring flowers and birdsong in the woods; October for fungi.

A battery-powered scooter can be provided on request.

The Old Park

Parkland

Weald Country Park

424ac/170ha   *CM14 5QS*   *TQ 570 939*

Essex County Council

This was a mediæval deer park and now is an attractive mix of semi-formal parkland with large blocks of woodland. The remnants of the deer park – its south-eastern quarter, called *The Park* – is scattered with massive oak and hornbeam pollards, some of which are probably more than 500 years old. Red Poll cattle graze here, and in parts it is rich in wild flowers, including unusual plants like heath violets and heath spotted orchids.

The woodland across the north was cleared during World War II and replanted in the 1950s and 1960s with native hardwood trees such as beech and oak. This has created some fine woodland that positively shimmers with bluebells in spring. Golden saxifage, an unusual ancient woodland plant, grows in Foxdown Wood, which escaped conifer planting.

Remnants of more recent landscaping survive also, in the form of the belvedere at the southern end, the avenue

Ancient hedgerow in the north of Weald Park

Weald Park lake in winter

From A12/M25 junction 28 take the A1023 towards Brentwood and turn left on to Wigley Bush Lane. This meets Weald Road in South Weald village, from which there are several entrances.

Regular bus services from Brentwood to Pilgrims Hatch. Occasional services to South Weald village.

Accessible at all times. Car parks open from dawn to dusk. Visitor centre open daily 10am–4pm weekdays, 9.30am–5pm on weekends.

April–May for bluebells and birdsong; July for flying insects and wild flowers in the damper parts.

Battery-powered scooters can be provided on request.

Parkland

of chestnut trees in the centre and the large ornamental lakes.

Such a variety of habitats attracts a wide variety of birds. Great crested grebes and moorhens breed on the lakes, and in winter flocks of seed-eating birds such as goldfinches and siskins can be seen feeding in the lakeside alders. Nuthatches and woodpeckers are often seen in the woods, and little owls can sometimes be seen hunting in the early evening.

Barry Small
Little owl *resident*

Parkland

Wanstead Park

200ac/81ha   E11 2LT   TQ 415 875

Once the renowned 18th-century gardens of Wanstead House, now Wanstead Park is managed by the City of London as part of Epping Forest. It has several large lakes, with secluded inlets, islands and marshy areas. These are surrounded by a mixture of mature woodland, parkland and open acid grassland where harebells grow. The River Roding runs along its eastern boundary.

This combination makes for rich wildlife, despite the constant visitor pressure. Birdlife is particularly good, with kingfishers seen regularly throughout the year, wildfowl visiting the lakes in winter and hobbies in summer, and both water birds and migrant warblers nesting in summer.

South of the A12 (Eastern Avenue)/M11 interchange. Can be reached from Wanstead Park Road to the east via an overbridge, from Woodlands Avenue/Northumberland Avenue to the south and from Warren Road to the north-west. No parking on the site.

Central line tube to Wanstead. Several bus services run to this station also.

Accessible in daylight hours only.

Autumn/winter for visiting wildfowl; April/May for woodland flowers and birdsong.

A good network of surfaced paths.

Brown hawker and blue-tailed damselfly *laying eggs in Perch Pond*

Harebell *flowers July–September*

Estuary and coast
Feeding groung for wintering birds

As the crow flies, the Essex coastline covers about 50 miles. Following every twist and turn of the many estuaries, islands and creeks, it is nearer 400 miles long. It is a mosaic of various habitats, from open sea, through the intertidal zone with saltmarsh and mudflats, to seawall and grazing marsh, plus some sand and shingle. Part of it, of course, has been developed for leisure and commerce, but what remains is a tremendous asset for wildlife and, specially, of international importance for wintering birds.

Holding back the sea

The seawalls surrounding most of the Essex coast today were constructed more than 300 years ago. Inside the seawall was a borrowdyke out of which the clay was excavated to build the wall. The land was predominantly saltmarsh and reclaiming it from the sea turned it into grassland. At the time this was usually grazed by sheep, and 100 years ago sheep were a common site on grazing marsh around the Essex coast.

Grazing marsh is a valuable habitat for plants, insects and breeding birds, but since then most coastal grazing marsh has been levelled, drained and ploughed to grow arable crops, losing most of its wildlife value. Most of the remaining grazing marsh is in the hands of conservation bodies, and managed for wildlife.

Sea level rise

The broad Essex estuaries are really drowned river valleys, formed by a process known as *isostatic adjustment.* Since the last Ice Age some 2.5 million years ago the north-west of

Sheep grazing at Blue House Farm, on the Crouch Estuary
Nick Robson

Estuary and coast

Eroding saltmarsh on the Essex coast
Chris Gomersall

Britain has been rising slowly because the huge weight of ice has been removed, and at the same time the south-east has been sinking. This has been reflected in a rise in sea level and, while historically the sea has been rising at around 3mm/year, currently the rate has increased to around 6mm/year as a result of the climate and the seas warming up.

Coastal squeeze

Sea level rise has led to a process known as *coastal squeeze*. Saltmarsh is a dynamic habitat that over the millennia has survived many variations in sea level by moving up- or down-slope, but when the rising sea pins it against hard defences such as a seawall it has nowhere to go and begins to erode. In the recent past 40% of Essex saltmarsh has been lost in this way.

Saltmarsh serves as a refuge and nursery for a wide range of aquatic life, and it also absorbs the power of the sea, so its loss increases the presssure on sea defences all around the coast. Combined with sea level rise, this dramatically increases the cost of sea defences, which have to be built higher and stronger year on year.

Coastal realignment

Government has concluded that the cost of maintaining all the current seawalls – including the 500km or so in Essex – will become unsustainable, and initiated a policy originally called *managed retreat*. This is the right term in the context of what has always been called *sea defence*, but it was seen as too defeatist in tone and has been replaced by the more neutral *coastal realignment*.

What it adds up to is that every stretch of seawall is evaluated. If the value of the assets it protects is high enough, such as if it protects housing or significant wildlife, the seawall will be maintained. If not, it will eventually be abandoned and the landowner compensated.

The first major coastal alignment project was carried out in 2002 at Essex Wildlife Trust's Abbotts Hall Farm, and since then there have been many similar projects all around the south and east coasts of England, recreating some of the lost intertidal habitats and coastal grassland.

Early stage of the coastal alignment project at Abbotts Hall Farm
Chris Gomersall

Estuary and coast 101

Wintering birds

Huge numbers of wildfowl and waders migrate to the Essex estuaries in autumn and winter to take advantage of the mild climate and abundant food supply, typically numbering around half-a-million birds. Species wintering here in internationally important numbers include brent goose, teal, grey plover and black- and bar-tailed godwits.

The brent goose in particular has been a conservation success story. Their numbers have recovered from dangerously low levels in the 1950s although they are still vulnerable. About one-fifth of the world population of 250,000 winters on the Essex coast, mainly along the Thames, Blackwater and Crouch estuaries.

They breed 2,500 miles away in Siberia and arrive here in mid-autumn, initially feeding on the eel-grass beds near Leigh-on-Sea before dispersing to other coastal sites. They start the return flight from late February on.

Black-tailed godwit
Alan Williams

Grey plover
Alan Williams

Brent geese

Abbotts Hall Farm

700ac/280ha   CO5 7RZ   TL 963 146   SSSI (part), SPA

This coastal farm was bought by Essex Wildlife Trust in 2000. It is the Trust's headquarters, and also a working farm rich in wildlife and a demonstration site for sustainable coastal defence.

Coastal realignment

The coastal realignment project at Abbotts Hall Farm was designed to recreate lost habitats by allowing sea water back on to the land reclaimed when the seawall was built. Two new counter walls were constructed at either end of the site to protect neighbouring land but elsewhere the land rises gently, checking the incoming tide without additional sea defenses. This has allowed the creation of 200 acres of mudflat, saltmarsh and coastal grassland.

The seawall was breached in five places in October 2002 and very quickly saltmarsh plants moved in. Other signs of marine life include shore crabs, jellyfish, lugworms and shrimps, and a number of fish species.

New grassland has been created between the developing saltmarsh and the remaining arable fields, and sheep are now back grazing as in they used to in the past.

Seven miles south of Colchester just off the B1026. From Colchester take the B1026 towards Maldon and turn off left towards Peldon about 3km beyond the causeway across Abberton Reservoir, or follow the B1026 from Maldon and keep straight on where it turns sharp left about 4km beyond Tolleshunt d'Arcy. The entrance is about 1km down on the right.

Open to the public Monday–Friday only, 9am–5pm.

Dogs are restricted to dog walk adjacent to main building.

This is a working farm and sometimes paths will be closed for safety reasons.

Estuary and coast

Wildlife-friendly farming

Over much of Essex, wildlife has been finding it more and more difficult to keep a foothold on the modern arable farm. Farmland birds such as grey partridge and corn bunting have experienced massive declines. The Trust is aiming to improve the lot of wildlife on the farm while continuing to grow food economically.

For over 30 years the previous cropping regime was dominated by wheat. Now the Trust is growing a wide range of crops, including wild bird seed mixes.

Conditions for wildlife have been improved in other ways by planting and coppicing hedges, leaving uncultivated field margins, and creating beetle banks across the centre of fields to encourage predatory insects.

Results have been good. The skylark population has increased along with many species of breeding bird, including yellowhammers, whitethroats and wagtails. Overwintering finches and thrushes feed on the food-rich field margins and in the hedgerows. Water voles breed on the stream and round the lake.

Many waders and wildfowl feed on the saltmarsh, and peregrine falcons and marsh harriers often fly through looking for prey. On the freshwater lake you may see water rail, kingfisher and little egret.

Sea lavender on Abbotts Hall Farm saltmarsh
Chris Gomersall

Casualties of modern farming:
Corn Bunting ...
David Harrison

... and Grey Partridge
Alan Williams

Estuary and coast

Blue House Farm

601ac/240ha   CM3 6GU   TQ 856 971   SSSI (part), SPA

Most of Blue House Farm was originally saltmarsh until seawalls were constructed to capture land from the sea. It was then used as grazing pasture, this practice continuing today. Some of the higher, drier fields were used for crops but have now reverted to grassland.

Its wildlife is internationally important, particularly overwintering birds and also coastal plants and insects. It is a working farm, managed by maintaining high water levels and balancing livestock farming with wildlife conservation.

The **flat fields** between the farmhouse and the seawall are used in winter as a feeding ground by brent geese. Sometimes more than 2,000 geese can be seen, grazing on the short turf. Throughout the year hares can be seen right across the farm, but most easily on these fields where cover is scarce. Skylarks nest in the hay fields in spring.

The deep water in the **fleets** attracts diving birds including tufted duck and little grebe.

Our smallest duck, the teal, and our largest, the shelduck, are both commonly seen here. At high tide wading birds move in from the mudflats beyond the sea wall.

Most of the pasture has never been ploughed and retains the features of the original saltmarsh, such as

Brown hare
Bob Glover

Estuary and coast

winding creeks and countless hollows and bumps often topped with the large anthills of the meadow ant.

The **marshy fields** to the south and east serve as a feeding ground for waders such as redshank, curlew and snipe. A large area near the railway is flooded every winter attracting many birds, and particularly wigeon and teal. As water levels drop in spring, bare mud rich in insects is exposed. Lapwing and redshank chicks thrive on insects and this has brought breeding lapwing and redshank back on to the farm.

The **creeks** and **ditches** are important habitats for rare water beetles and other insects like the hairy dragonfly and scarce emerald damselfly. Those with thick vegetation support water voles.

The **former arable** is now grazed and supports breeding yellow wagtails and corn buntings, plus the occasional grey partridge.

The **saltmarsh** and **intertidal mud** between seawall and river provide food for wading birds such as oystercatcher and black-tailed godwit. In the river itself you will often see red-breasted merganser and cormorant and occasionally common seal, feeding on the rich marine life of the estuary.

Take the B1012 east from South Woodham Ferrers and after about 3 miles turn right to North Fambridge. Access is via a track on the left off Fambridge Road 400m south of North Fambridge station.

A regular train service runs to Fambridge via Wickford.

Accessible at all times.

Mid-October to March for brent geese and wintering wildfowl; April–June for breeding birds and for hares.

No dogs on the permissive footpath, and please keep them under strict control elsewhere.

Please close gates behind you as this is a working farm as well as a nature reserve.

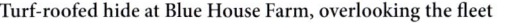

Turf-roofed hide at Blue House Farm, overlooking the fleet
Nick Robson

Estuary and coast

Bowers Marsh

667ac/270ha   SS13 2EZ   TQ 755 867

Bowers Marsh is former grazing marsh, drained 60 or so years ago to grow arable crops. Acquired by RSPB with support from Veolia, who operate the tip nearby, water levels have been raised to create freshwater and saline lagoons and to reinvigorate the original ditches, which now are lined with reeds and other aquatic plants.

Large numbers of birds occupy the lagoons and wet flushes in winter. Most noticeable are the gulls, resting from feeding on the tip nearby, alongside large flocks of lapwing, and some teal and shoveler. Flocks of geese and wigeon feed on the grassland. Such a quantity of potential prey attracts raptors such as marsh harriers.

In spring, lapwings display and skylarks spiral up in song as they prepare to breed. Cetti's and reed warblers nest along the ditches, and in summer dragonflies such as four-spotted chaser and ruddy darter emerge.

South-east of Pitsea, reached via Church Lane, which turns south off London Road (B1464) about 1km east of Pitsea.

Two miles from Pitsea station (Fenchurch St line) – turn right out of Station Approach then right into Brackendale Avenue, then follow the footpath beside the railway to Church Road, turning right down to the reserve.

Accessible at all times. Car park open daily 9am to 5pm except Xmas Day, Boxing Day and New Year.

Mid-October to March for wintering birds; April–June for breeding birds; summer for flying insects.

No dogs allowed except assistance dogs. On public footpaths please keep dogs on leads.

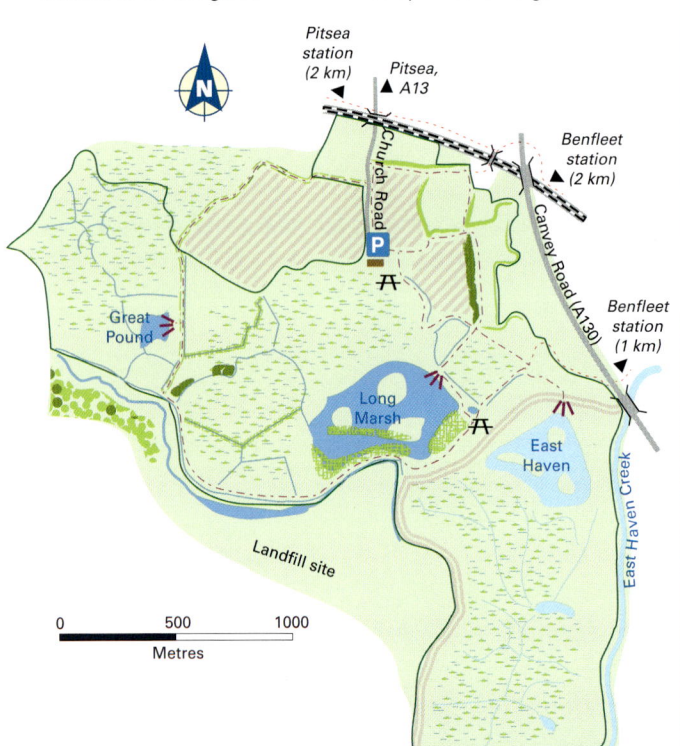

Reed warbler *summer visitor*
David Harrison

Estuary and coast 107

Alan Williams
Lapwing *partial resident*

Four-spotted chaser *female, flies June–mid-August*

Lapwing and gulls on the saline lagoon, East Haven *with the landfill site and port behind*

Estuary and coast

Bradwell Shell Bank

200ac/80ha **CM0 7PW** **TM 035 081** **SSSI, SPA, SAC**

This nature reserve on the Dengie peninsula consists of some 30 acres of shell bank, together with extensive saltmarsh. The shell bank is continuous between Tip Head and Gunner's Creek, but further south consists of a series of small cockle spits, many of which are separated by deep creeks and gullies. The adjoining saltmarsh in some places is several hundred metres wide.

Ringed plovers and oystercatchers breed on the shell banks, and the saltmarsh supports many species including redshank, yellow wagtail, meadow pipit, reed bunting and linnet. In autumn and winter large flocks of up to 20,000 waders roost on the reserve at high tide.

Raptors hunting over the area include hen harrier, merlin, peregrine and short-eared owl in winter; marsh harrier, sparrowhawk and hobby at other times.

The more stable parts of the shell banks are rich in flowers, including yellow horned-poppy, sea rocket, sea holly and sea kale.

Ringed plover *resident*
Alan Williams

The mud and sandflats to the east of the reserve, extending some 3km from the shore, are part of the Dengie National Nature Reserve. These are internationally important for overwintering waders, and notably for grey

Oystercatcher *resident*
Alan Williams

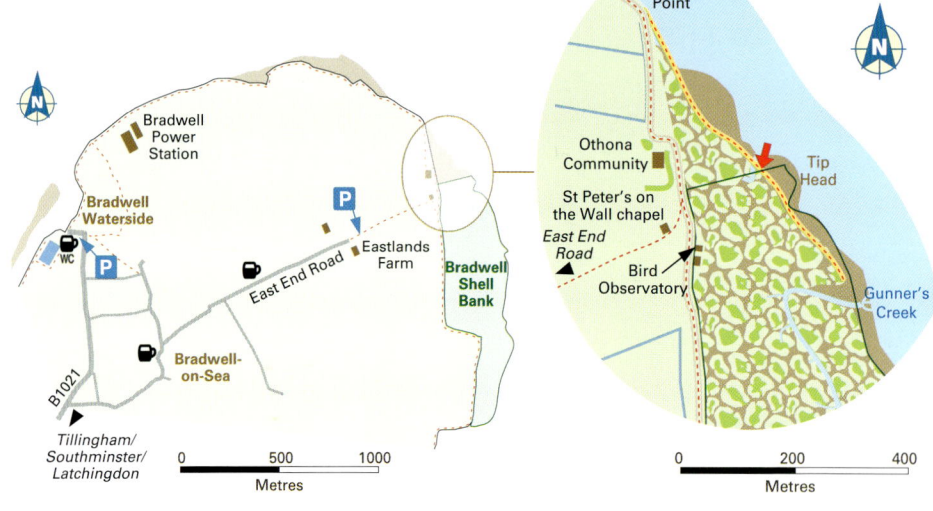

plover, knot and bar-tailed godwit. From Sales Point you can watch the birds feeding, ideally when the tide is rising to cover the mudflats. As well as those already mentioned, you may see dunlin, redshank, oystercatcher and curlew.

Continue north along the seawall path and you may also find turnstone, sanderling and ringed plover. Flocks of brent geese could be on the fields, the mud or the sea. The small thicket between the Bird Observatory and Sales Point is used as a refuge by many migrating birds.

The barges sunk just offshore are there to protect the saltmarsh and seawall from erosion.

Head for Bradwell-on-Sea via Latchingdon or Southminster, following the B1010/B1018/B1021 from Chelmsford or Maldon. Turn right in Bradwell by the church to follow East End Road to its end and park at Eastlands Farm. The reserve is entered via the Saxon chapel of St Peter's on the Wall – a distance of about 800m from there. To reach the reserve, walk northwards along the seawall to Sales Point, then southwards along the public beach to Tip Head Creek. This can be crossed quite easily at low tide and gives access to the first few hundred yards of the reserve, as far south as Gunners' Creek. *This creek is wide, with deep mud in parts, and no attempt should be made to cross it!*

Accessible at all times. To see waders, time your visit to coincide with high tide. At Bradwell this is just before Southend and about 90 minutes before London Bridge.

Winter for waders and wildfowl; summer for coastal wild flowers; migration periods for rarities.

Access for the disabled can be arranged through the warden: call Essex Wildlife Trust on 01621 862960.

To protect breeding shorebirds, between April and August inclusive please keep to the seawall overlooking the reserve, or where no wall exists to the edge of the saltmarsh.

Saxon chapel at Bradwell

Estuary and coast

Colne Point

683ac/273ha   CO16 8ET   TM 108 125   NNR, SSSI, SPA

This large reserve at the mouth of the Colne Estuary consists of a shingle ridge enclosing a considerable area of saltmarsh. The shingle and sand is nearly all that remains of a much larger area between Walton-on-the-Naze and St Osyth that existed at the end of the 19th century but has now mostly been developed by the holiday industry.

It is of special interest if you want to explore the development of shingle structures, because it is the best developed spit on the Essex coast and illustrates the various stages of stabilisation.

It is rich in plants and animals, including many rarities. The saltmarsh has golden samphire, and the shingle ridge sea holly, sea bindweed, sea spurge, yellow horned-poppy and sea kale.

In autumn and winter the mudflats serve as a feeding ground for large numbers of waders, with geese and ducks feeding on the saltmarsh and grebes and divers offshore.

It is a major migration route and in autumn when the weather conditions are right birds constantly stream through. In summer oystercatcher, ringed plover and redshank nest here.

 Access from St Osyth via Lee Wick Road.

Accessible at all times, but note that parts of the reserve can be flooded during very high tides, including around the car park and either end of the footbridge, so check the tide tables before you visit.

Migration periods for birds; summer for saltmarsh plants and insects.

Dogs not permitted.

During the breeding season (March to September) please walk below the last high tide mark as eggs and chicks are extremely difficult to see and are easily trampled.

Wellies or waterproof boots advisable as it may be muddy, or even necessary to wade, at any time of year.

Golden samphire
flowers August–September

Estuary and coast

Colne LNR

67ac/27a **CO7 9GW** **TM 034 217** **LNR, SSSI (part)**

Colchester

This Local Nature Reserve on the east bank of the River Colne includes Wivenhoe Wood, a fine old coppice woodland with many sweet chestnut trees, alongside grassland and scrub that once belonged to Lower Lodge Farm, a section of tidal foreshore with saltmarsh, and at the southern end an area of former grazing marsh.

Reed and sedge warblers nest in the marshland and whitethroats in the scrub. An area of saltmarsh to the west of the railway line can be reached via a level crossing and is used by wading birds such as redshank.

From the sea wall path there are good views of the inner estuary of the Colne and over the ditches, dykes and ponds of the marsh. Unusual plants like strawberry clover and slender hare's-ear grow here, and it has a rich insect life, with many dragonflies and damselflies on the wing in summer and stag beetles blundering in from Wivenhoe Wood to the north.

Stag beetle *male, best seen May/June*

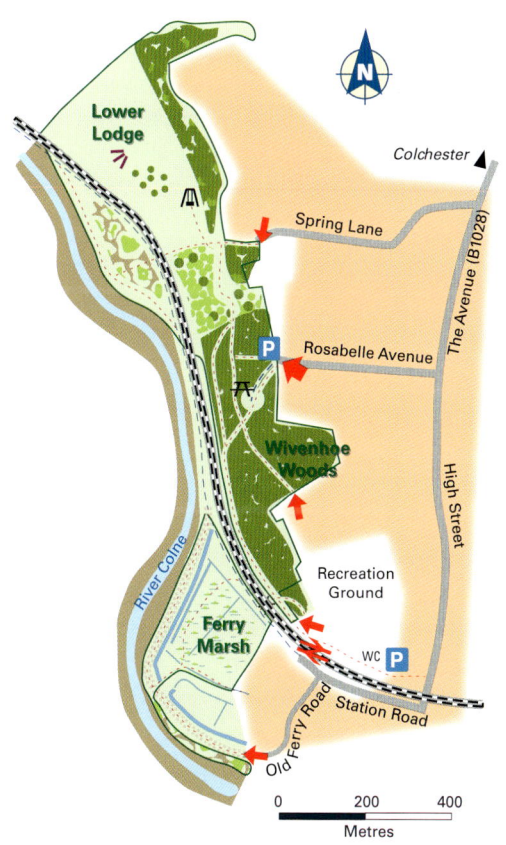

Access via Rosabelle Avenue, a turning off the B1028 north of Wivenhoe centre, or from the south via the sea wall path or public footpaths alongside the railway.

Wivenhoe station is not far from the southern end of the LNR. Regular buses run from Colchester to Wivenhoe.

Accessible at all times.

May/June for birdsong in the woods and scrub; July/August for insects along the woodland edge and in clearings, and around the marsh and foreshore.

A surfaced path runs from the car park at the end of Rosabelle Avenue to the picnic site. The footpath west of the railway is surfaced also.

Cudmore Grove Country Park

35ac/14ha   **CO5 8UE**   **TM 055 147**   **NNR, SSSI, SPA**   Essex County Council

This country park takes its name from a small grove of trees growing on the cliff top. This was the only woodland on Mersea Island, but some of it has been lost as the sea has worn away the soft sands and gravels of the cliff, which contains fossils dating back 300,000 years.

It is mainly grassland. Some areas of grass are left long throughout the year, others are cut for hay in June, and on summer days many species of butterfly can be seen feeding on meadows and hedgerows. Common seals can occasionally be seen along the Colne estuary.

The country park and the Colne Estuary National Nature Reserve alongside are really exceptional for birdlife in winter. The damp pastures at the northern end are managed for brent geese, and also attract golden plover and snipe in winter. Follow the seawall path beyond them and you are likely to see birds all around you – waders feeding on the mudflats, songbirds finding cover in the saltmarsh, and sea ducks like goldeneye and red-breasted merganser on the estuary.

Another special attraction of Mersea Island is that red squirrels have successfully been reintroduced there.

Exposed gravels in the cliffs

Estuary and coast   **113**

Cudmore Grove pond *with flooded fields behind*

⊕ Bear left to East Mersea after crossing The Strood on to Mersea Island (B1025 from Colchester). The country park is beyond East Mersea village, off Bromans Lane.

🕒 Open from 8am until dusk, all the year round.

🎟 January/February for waders and wildfowl; July for butterflies and saltmarsh colours.

♿ Mainly flat with easy walking ground mostly accessible by wheelchair.

📋 The access road – The Strood – is sometimes covered by spring tides.

Flowers of the sea shore

Sea pea *flowers June–July*

Sea bindweed *flowers June–August*)
Adrian Knowles

Sea rocket *flowers June–September*

Sea holly *powder-blue flowers June–September*

Sea kale *white flowers May–August*

Yellow horned-poppy
flowers June–September
Jonathan Smith

Fingringhoe Wick

125ac/50ha   *CO5 7DN*   *TM 041 195*   *SSSI, SPA (part)*

Fingringhoe Wick on the west shore of the Colne Estuary is one of Essex Wildlife Trust's top reserves. It has been created out of disused gravel workings and has a wide range of habitats, including patches of grassland, gorse heathland, mixed woodland, reedbeds, ponds and a large lake. The river frontage has saltmarsh, foreshore and intertidal mudflats. It is on sloping ground overlooking the Colne Estuary, offering one of the finest saltmarsh panoramas in eastern England.

In 2015 the seawall was breached to allow the sea back into land just north of the original reserve, creating more than 50 acres of new intertidal habitat, which was quickly colonised by saltmarsh plants and birds.

With such a wide range of habitats it supports a huge variety of wildlife. The highlight is probably the mass nightingale chorus in spring – typically 30 to 40 pairs nest. Other breeding birds include kestrels, tawny owls, little grebes and sparrowhawks. Between June and September, migrant waders use The Scrape. The estuary, quiet for much of the year, comes into its own in winter. Thousands of wintering waders and wildfowl rely on the expanses of mud and saltmarsh for food or for roosting, with sometimes as many as 700 avocets.

It is a special place for raptors – marsh harriers, buzzards and peregrines are seen regularly; barn, tawny and little owls quite often; and merlin and hen harrier visit in winter.

Three miles south-east of Colchester. Follow the B1025 from Colchester towards Mersea and, after crossing the Roman River, turn first left and follow the brown signs to the reserve. The lanes between Fingringhoe village and the reserve are narrow – please drive with caution.

Open daily from 9am–5pm, excluding Christmas Day and Boxing Day. Day permits must be obtained from the centre. Donations invited from non-members of the Trust: £2 for adults, £1 for children and £5 for families (2 adults and 2 children).

Worth visiting at any time of the year, but the highlights are the nightingale chorus in May and the flocks of wildfowl and waders in winter.

A short nature trail (leaflet available) is suitable for people in wheelchairs. Two bird hides that overlook the lake have concrete access paths and low-level viewing slots. A wheelchair is available in the centre on request.

Dogs are permitted on site, but must be kept to the dog trail and be on a lead at all times.

East Heath
Laurie Forsyth

Estuary and coast

It has a wide range of flowering plants, including common spotted orchids and bee orchids. Summer is best for colourful species, especially sea lavender on the saltmarsh, and masses of dog roses. The shaded, humid conditions in the thickets suit ferns, mosses and lichens.

Many species of dragonfly and damselfly breed on the reserve, as do many common butterflies, together with the less usual green hairstreak. The sandy, eroding cliff faces attract bees, ants and wasps.

Common lizards, slow worms, great crested newts and smooth newts are abundant, and adders and grass snakes are seen regularly. Water voles can be seen in some of the ponds.

The Geedon Saltmarsh
Laurie Forsyth

Nightingale: many nest here
Kev Chapman

Estuary and coast

Hadleigh Hadleigh country park

Essex County Council

300ac/121ha   SS7 2PP   TQ 799 870

This country park is hillside running down, steeply in places, to grazing marsh, seawall and a narrow strip of saltmarsh alongside Benfleet Creek.

The hillside has a mosaic of grassland, scrub and light woodland. The hay meadows and rides are full of flowers such as rest-harrow, birdsfoot trefoil and self-heal, and also support some unusual plants, including deptford pink, bithynian vetch and wild catmint.

On sunny summer days butterflies such as comma, speckled wood and skippers flutter along the rides, and adders slither out to sun themselves. Benfleet Downs is particularly rich in insects, including a national rarity, the shrill carder bee.

Cattle graze the marshland behind the seawall. In summer meadow pipits and skylarks nest here and it is alive with insects, including scarce emerald damselflies. Little grebes and reed warblers breed along the dykes and ponds.

Entrance via Chapel Lane, which leaves the A13 by the Morrison's supermarket in Hadleigh.

Benfleet station (Fenchurch St line) is a short walk from the western arm of the park. Bus services run along the A13 through Hadleigh and to Benfleet station.

Open from 8am until dusk all year round.

Mid-summer for wild flowers, butterflies and other insects; winter for birds, ideally at high tide when they are closest.

Scarce emerald damselfly *flies July–August*
Ted Benton

Estuary and coast

Two Tree Island

641ac/260ha **SS9 2GB** **TQ 824 852** **SSSI, NNR**

ESSEX Wildlife Trust

Two Tree Island was reclaimed from the sea in the 18th century when a seawall was built around saltmarsh. It was used for rough grazing until 1910, then as a rubbish tip until the 1970s.

It consists of grassland, scrub, reedbed and lagoons, and attracts a wide variety of birds, and particularly migrants. During the winter short-eared owls visit, hunting for field voles, and large numbers of little egrets roost here. Water vole, kingfisher, water rail, reed and sedge warblers may be seen in the lagoons and reedbed.

At its western end is a lagoon with a bird hide, from which you can often see birds such as redshank and heron feeding. Avocets usually nest here also.

The eastern section forms part of the Leigh National Nature Reserve, which extends eastwards to include Leigh Sands. This is an important area for migratory birds, and includes large beds of eelgrass, which brent geese feast on after their arrival in autumn.

Avocet resident
David Harrison

Turn south off the A13 down to Leigh station, then cross the bridge over the railway and follow the road past the golf range and over the bridge on to the island. There is a car park immediately over the bridge.

Twenty minutes' walk from Leigh station (Fenchurch St line), which is also served by a number of bus services.

Accessible at all times.

Migration periods and winter for birds – brent geese normally present from late September to mid-November; July for saltmarsh colours and butterflies.

To avoid disturbing the birds, please keep strictly to the marked footpaths in the eastern section.

Estuary and coast

Rainham Marshes

870ac/352ha   **RM19 1SZ**   **TQ 552 792**   **SSSI**

In 2000 the RSPB acquired Aveley and Wennington Marshes, formerly used by the Ministry of Defence as a firing range and a substantial part of the Inner Thames Marshes SSSI, and has developed it into a fine nature reserve.

Some 20km of ditch have been restored and sluices have been installed to control water levels across the reserve. Scrapes – areas of shallow water – have been constructed to provide habitat for breeding waders and wintering waterfowl. The ditches also act as wet fences so that the grassland can be grazed without intrusive fencing.

Such a large area of grazing marsh adjacent to the Thames Estuary is very important in wildlife terms and particularly for its birds. Large numbers of wildfowl winter here, with wigeon regularly reaching 1,000 and teal up to 3,500. The reserve also supports important numbers of breeding

Estuary and coast

reed bunting, little grebe, meadow pipit and skylark, with stonechat, barn owl, grasshopper warbler and water rail also breeding.

On the Thames nearby, large numbers of dunlin and black-tailed godwits winter, along with curlew, grey plover and turnstone.

The reserve also has a large population of water voles and many unusual plants and invertebrates. Its noisiest resident is the marsh frog, introduced into Kent from mainland Europe in the 1930s and now spreading across southern England.

The Environment and Education centre contains a café and shop and provides good views across the marshes and River Thames. It has been built to high environmental standards, with features such as solar panels, rainwater harvesting, natural light and ventilation and a ground source heat pump.

From M25 junct 30 head west along the A13 to its junction with the A1306 and follow the A1306 south towards Purfleet. Turn right at the traffic lights on to New Tank Hill Road. The entrance is on the right 300m down.

Nearest rail station is Purfleet (Fenchurch St line). Turn right outside the station and follow the road to 'The Royal', on the left, then head down to the Thames and join the Riverside Path. This crosses the Mardyke River at a small bridge, after which turn left and follow the path round to the centre.

Open 9.30am to 4.30pm daily. Free access to RSPB members and residents of Havering and Thurrock; otherwise £2.50/adult, £1/child.

Something of interest at all times of the year: highlights are large movements of migrating birds in autumn and large flocks of wildfowl and waders in winter.

Paths and trails are suitable for wheelchairs

Reed bunting *male, resident*
Alan Williams

Marsh frog

Rainham Marshes seen from the seawall
mattbuck

South Woodham Ferrers

On the Crouch Estuary, right next to South Woodham Ferrers new town, is a large area of coastal marshland that has been set aside as Marsh Farm Country Park. A mile or so north of the country park via a walk along the seawall is Woodham Fen, an Essex Wildlife Trust nature reserve.

Woodham Fen

20ac/8ha   CM3 5XH   TQ 798 975   SSSI, SPA

This is former common land between and near the tidal limits of two small creeks running south into the River Crouch. The southern part is saltmarsh and the northern rough grassland with a transitional zone between the two – of special interest because this natural transition is now very unusual in Essex. It has a wide range of saltmarsh plants, including sea wormwood, and the grassland is full of wild flowers, including slender birdsfoot trefoil, grass vetchling and wild carrot.

It attracts many breeding birds, including reed bunting, yellow wagtail and meadow pipit, and a variety of small waders occur on passage. Teal, snipe and rock pipit can be seen in winter, when kingfishers hunt along the creeks for eels. Barn owls and other birds of prey hunt over the grassland for the many field voles.

Essex skipper and a number of the other common butterflies are abundant, as are common lizards and slow worms.

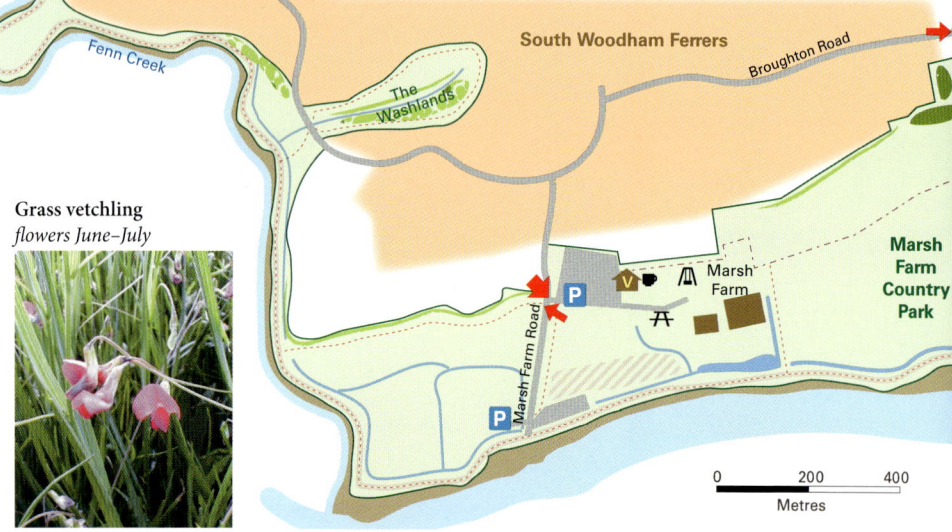

Grass vetchling
flowers June–July

Estuary and coast

Marsh Farm country park

350ac/140ha   *CM3 5WP*   *TQ 810 961*   *SSSI, SPA*

Essex County Council

Essex County Council operates Marsh Farm on a semi-commercial basis, raising cattle, sheep and other animals, and both the farm and the surrounding grazing marsh are open to the public, with a small charge for entry to the farm.

The grazing marsh has a long history going back to the 18th century. Part of its seawall was breached during the 'Great Flood' of 1953 and the remains are still visible from the new wall built further back.

The nature reserve towards the eastern end consists of rough grassland, saltmarsh and a scrape – a shallow water lagoon. Hares are often about in the grassland and reed buntings nest along the dykes. The scrape attracts many wildfowl in winter and at migration periods, and especially wigeon and teal.

Shelduck, dunlin and redshank feed in Clementsgreen Creek when the mud is exposed. In winter brent geese graze the fields west of the entrance and you may see flocks of snow buntings along the seawall.

Enter Woodham Fen from the A132 at the roundabout where it meets the B1012. To reach Marsh Farm turn right down Ferrers Road and follow Inchbonnie Road round to Marsh Farm Road.

The station is about five minutes' walk from Woodham Fen via a footpath, and two miles from Marsh Farm via the creekside path. Bus services run to and from Chelmsford, Wickford and Basildon.

Accessible at all times via footpaths. Marsh Farm visitor centre open daily March–October, otherwise weekends only; 10am–5.30pm weekends, bank holidays and in summer, otherwise 10am–4.30pm. Visitor centre car park open 9am–6pm; riverside car park 8am–dusk.

Midsummer onwards for wild flowers and butterflies; migration periods and winter for birds.

Paths can be very muddy in winter.

Snow bunting *winter visitor*

Estuary and coast

The Naze

Tendring District Council

137ac/55ha   **CO14 8LE**   **TM 264 235**   **SSSI (part)**

The Naze is from the Old English *naes*, meaning a nose. It is a headland roughly three miles long and one mile wide, stretching northwards from the town of Walton-on-the-Naze. Behind it is Hamford Water, which it shelters from the North Sea. At its southern end is a hill that is being eroded, with the result that 20-metre high cliffs rise directly from the beach – unique on the Essex coast.

The cliffs are important geologically because of a spectacular exposure of a sandy deposit called Red Crag, formed about 3 million years ago when the sea covered most of Essex and containing large numbers of fossils. Red Crag erodes easily. Two concrete pillboxes lying out on the beach show how quickly erosion is occuring: they were built on the clifftop during World War II.

In summer the cliffs provide secure sites for the nesting holes of sand martins. The large gorse bushes and elder scrub on top of the cliff provide cover for small birds such as linnets and goldfinches, as do the taller plants growing on the fallen cliff material at its foot. Waders, gulls and terns can be seen along the shore.

During migration periods it is a prime birdwatching site. Curlew sandpipers are seen along the beach regularly, with gannets and arctic skuas passing offshore. With east winds blowing, small birds such as firecrest and black redstart may be found sheltering in the bushes on the clifftop.

Head northwards along the coast road through Walton. By the Eastcliffe Hotel take the left fork and follow Hall Lane and Naze Park Road for about a mile.

Regular buses run from Clacton and Frinton via Walton station (train link to Colchester) and from the bus station on the front.

Accessible at all times.

April–June for early flowers and birdsong; autumn for migrating birds.

Please keep dogs under close control in John Weston reserve.

Beware fast-incoming tides when walking to Stone Point.

A mile-long shingle beach stretches forwards from the tip of the Naze, ending at Stone Point. This is an important nesting site for little terns and other birds like oystercatchers and ringed plovers. It is cordoned off in the breeding season to prevent disturbance.

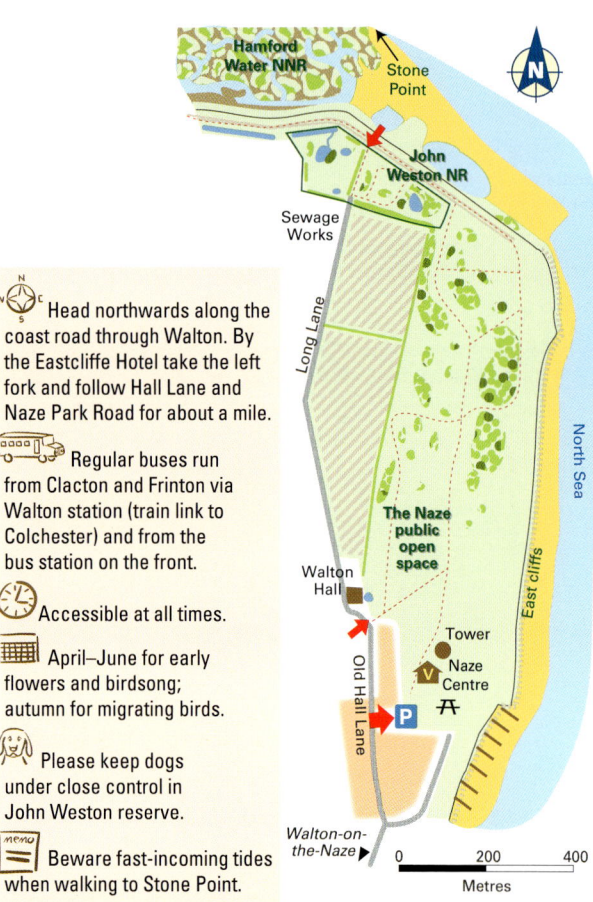

John Weston nature reserve

9ac/4ha   *CO14 8LE*   *TM 266 245*   *SSSI*

This nature reserve at the northern end of the Naze consists of blackthorn and bramble thickets, rough grassland and four ponds or 'scrapes'. It is named after a leading Essex naturalist and former warden of the reserve.

Its nesting birds include cetti's warbler and both common and lesser whitethroat. Water rail are seen and heard regularly. It is an important landfall for migrants and also attracts a variety of winter visitors.

Notable among its flowering plants are parsley water-dropwort, slender thistle, pepper saxifrage and fenugreek.

A circular path runs around the eastern section and is good for butterflies and other insects in summer.

Pepper saxifrage *fl. July–August*

Eroding cliffs at The Naze
Paul Farmer

Tollesbury Wick

599ac/240ha   **CM9 8RY**   **TL 970 104**   **SSSI, SPA**

This is a rare example of an Essex freshwater grazing marsh, worked for decades by traditional methods sympathetic to wildlife. Now it is grazed by rare breed sheep and cattle, and water levels are managed to create good conditions for wildlife.

Its 600 acres of rough pasture, borrowdykes, seawalls, wet flushes, pools and saltmarsh are full of wildlife. Large areas of rough pasture suit small mammals such as field vole and pygmy shrew. In winter, they in turn attract hunting hen harriers and short-eared owls.

Dry grassland on the slopes of the seawalls supports spiny restharrow, grass vetchling, slender hare's-ear and many other wild flowers.

Borrowdykes trace the inland edge of the seawall for its entire length. Reed warbler and reed bunting nest in them in spring, and all year

Follow the B1023 to Tollesbury, then follow Woodrolfe Road towards the marina and car park.

Bus services run to Tollesbury from Maldon, Colchester and Witham.

Accessible at all times along the seawall footpath.

Suitable for motorised wheelchair access up to Blockhouse Bay.

July for saltmarsh colours and for insects; winter for wildfowl and waders.

Sheep ticks can be a problem in April–June: keep out of the long grass.

Estuary and coast

Christian Fisher
Spiny restharrow *fl. July–August*

Alan Williams
Little grebe *male in breeding plumage, resident*

heron and little grebe search them for food. Wet flushes, dykes and small pools in the pasture support aquatic plants such as water crowfoot, and dragonflies breed there.

Golden plover, lapwing, brent geese and wigeon feed or roost on the wet grassland in winter.

Outside the seawall, creeks, saltmarsh and exposed mud support coastal birds and saltmarsh flowers. Shinglehead Point has yellow horned-poppy and also a small colony of one of Britain's scarcest breeding birds, little terns.

View across Woodrolfe Creek towards West Mersea
Glyn Baker

126 Estuary and coast

Wallasea Island

635ac/257ha   **SS4 2HD**   **TQ 945 946**

Wallasea Island is the site of RSPB's Wild Coast Project. Previously arable farmland enclosed within a seawall, starting in 2010 spoil from the Crossrail project was imported to recreate large areas of coastal habitat such as existed here before the seawall was built. Development will continue until 2025, and the map shows the state of play in 2019.

In winter thousands of wildfowl and waders can be expected to colonise the new habitats RSPB is creating. Expect to see dunlin, grey plover, redshank, turnstone and curlew feeding on the mud or roosting on the islands; shelduck, mallard, teal and wigeon on the open water; grey heron and little egret around the fringes; stonechats and meadow pipits in the drier grassland; and flocks of lapwing and golden plover on the grazing marsh.

Wallasea Island panorama
Glyn Baker

Estuary and coast

Such large congregations of birds attract many raptors: marsh harrier, peregrine, merlin and kestrel all year, short-eared owl and hen harrier in winter.

Bird numbers will be much fewer in spring and summer – skylarks nesting in the drier grassland; reed buntings along the borrowdykes; corn buntings, whitethroats and linnets around the bird cover.

There are lots of brown hares, and an area specially designed for water voles south of Marsh Flats.

Earlier, in 2006, a series of lagoons were created by DEFRA along the northern edge of the island as compensation for habitat lost to development elsewhere. You can get good views of these from the footpath along the seawall.

From Rochford, take the Ashingdon Road and turn right into Brays Lane. Follow the brown tourist signs from there, along Apton Hall Road and then Creeksea Ferry Road.

Train to Burnham and ferry from there (Easter to end September). Phone 07704 060482 for details and to book.

Accessible at all times. Car park open 8am to dusk or 7.30pm.

Spring for nesting birds; July for saltmarsh colours and for insects; winter for wildfowl and waders.

Dogs allowed only on the seawall footpath.

Birds on Pool Marsh in winter

Raptors that you may see here, hunting for prey...

Kestrel *resident*

Alan Williams

Short-eared owl *winter visitor*

Alan Williams

Merlin *partial migrant*

Alan Williams

Estuary and coast

West Canvey Marshes

635ac/257ha SS8 0QA TQ 770 845

RSPB manages this large area of coastal grazing marsh principally for breeding waders such as lapwings and redshanks, using a mix of cattle grazing and hay cutting, plus control of water levels. The saltmarsh alongside Benfleet Creek has the highest density of breeding redshanks in Essex.

The north and west sides of the reserve are bounded by tidal creeks frequented by oystercatchers, knots, dunlins, godwits and sandpipers. The wide fleet, with its open water and fringe of reeds, attracts good numbers of feeding little egrets. In summer, skylarks nest in the drier grassland and the scrubby areas attract linnets and whitethroats.

Summer also brings good numbers of butterflies, dragonflies and other insects.

Water voles and a large great crested newt colony occupy the freshwater ditches.

After crossing on to Canvey Island via the A130, turn right at the first roundabout on to Canvey Road. The car park is on the right at the next roundabout.

Buses run from Benfleet station past the reserve entrance.

Accessible at all times.

May–June for breeding birds; July–August for butterflies and dragonflies.

The fleet on West Canvey Marshes
Hugh Venables

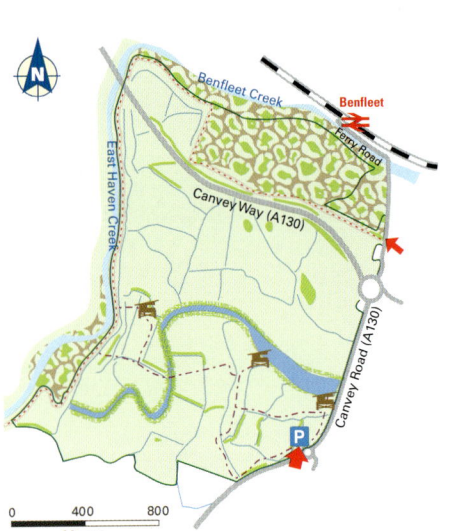

Redshank *resident, many nest here*
David Harrison

Rivers and wetlands
Fresh water for wildlife

Healthy rivers are vital for a wide range of wildlife, from otters and kingfishers near the top of the food chain, down to tiny aquatic creatures at the bottom. With stricter controls on pollution Essex rivers have been cleaned up recently, and as a result otters have returned to many of their former haunts.

Draining the wetlands

Yet many rivers, and especially urban rivers, have been canalised to 'tidy them up' and to protect against floods. Even where still natural, they have often been confined between levées so that adjoining land – floodplain land – could be used for grazing and sometimes even housing.

This is part of a long history of wetland drainage in East Anglia, on a large scale in the case of the Norfolk fens and on a small but widespread scale along many rivers. As a result many of the wetlands – fens, marshes and wet meadows – normally associated with them have been lost, together with their wildlife.

Rivers and wetlands

Natural flood management

As well as supporting wildlife, wetlands perform another valuable function: by holding up water within the catchment they knock the peaks off high flows and reduce the risk of flooding downstream. This has been recognised by Environment Agency in its policy of *natural flood management*, which means naturalising rivers to slow down flows and allowing flood water to overflow on to the floodplain where it will cause no significant damage.

It is a recognition, as along the coast, of the limitations of hard defences in an era of climate change and extreme weather events, and has also thrown wetlands a lifeline. The best of the few remaining in Essex are included here. Hopefully there will be more to include in future editions.

Wetland wildlife

Dragonflies and damselflies are the most noticeable wetland residents in summer, emerging to spend a few weeks as adults after months or years developing under water. Common blue damselflies, ruddy darters and broad-bodied chasers can be seen almost anywhere there is fresh water and plenty of aquatic vegetation, most conspicuous coupled in mating pairs, or laying eggs by dipping their tails into the water.

Water voles have been lost from many rivers due to habitat loss and predation by american mink, originally released from fur farms and now widespread in Britain. Otters subsist mainly on fish, but mink are less choosy and can wipe out a wide range of native wetland wildlife, including water voles, a short time after they become established. Thanks to determined efforts to control invading mink, water voles are still present on many Essex rivers.

Kingfishers, like otters, live mainly on fish, so they too are symbols of clean rivers. You are most likely to see them sitting on a favourite perch over the water, watching for fish, or flying rapidly across the water like an electric blue dart.

Otter *now returning to Essex rivers*

Common blue damselfly
male; flies June–August

Ruddy darters mating
male above; flies August–September

Kingfisher *resident*

Rivers and wetlands

Beam Valley

The Beam Valley separates the London Borough of Havering from Barking & Dagenham to the west. It forms part of the Dagenham Corridor, a green corridor that extends all the way through eastern London from rural Essex to the Thames and serves as a valuable flyway for migrating birds.

The Chase nature reserve

The London Borough of Barking & Dagenham

120ac/49ha   RM7 0SS   TQ 515 860   LNR

This nature reserve is former gravel workings. When extraction finished in the late 1960s some of the pits escaped infilling and formed a valuable wetland habitat of seasonal ponds, lakes and marshes.

The Chase is of interest principally for its birds. Kingfisher, skylark, little ringed plover and lapwing all breed here. Teal, snipe and shoveler visit in winter.

The River Rom flows down its eastern fringe. This stretch has been straightened and deepened at both ends but in between it meanders in a natural channel and supports water voles.

The grassland is moderately rich in flowers including some unusual ones such as spiny restharrow and haresfoot clover. At its southern end it is grazed by horses.

Signposted from Dagenham Road which runs south from Rush Green Road (A124 Upminster–Hornchurch–Dagenham). Pedestrian access from Upper Rainham Road, parking beside the road.

15-minute walk from Dagenham East tube station (see map overleaf).

Accessible at all times. Car parks open dawn till dusk.

May for breeding birds, with gorse and hawthorn in flower; September to March for birds on passage and wintering in the reserve.

To avoid disturbing the birds, please do not go inside the fence around The Slack and keep dogs under strict control.

Little ringed plover *summer visitor*
Andreas Trepte

Snipe *resident*
Alan Williams

Eastbrookend Country Park

The London Borough of Barking & Dagenham

188ac/76ha   RM7 0SS   TQ 510 860

This extensive country park was created on land between Dagenham and Hornchurch damaged by gravel extraction, opening in 1995. Groups of trees have been planted which are now maturing and it has a number of lakes and ponds.

Fels Fields to the north of Dagenham Road has large grassland areas frequented by skylarks and meadow pipits. Eastbrook Grove to the south houses the visitor centre and has several large water bodies, where ducks, grebes and coots nest. The eastern section, adjoining The Chase nature reserve, has a heath-like character.

Rivers and wetlands

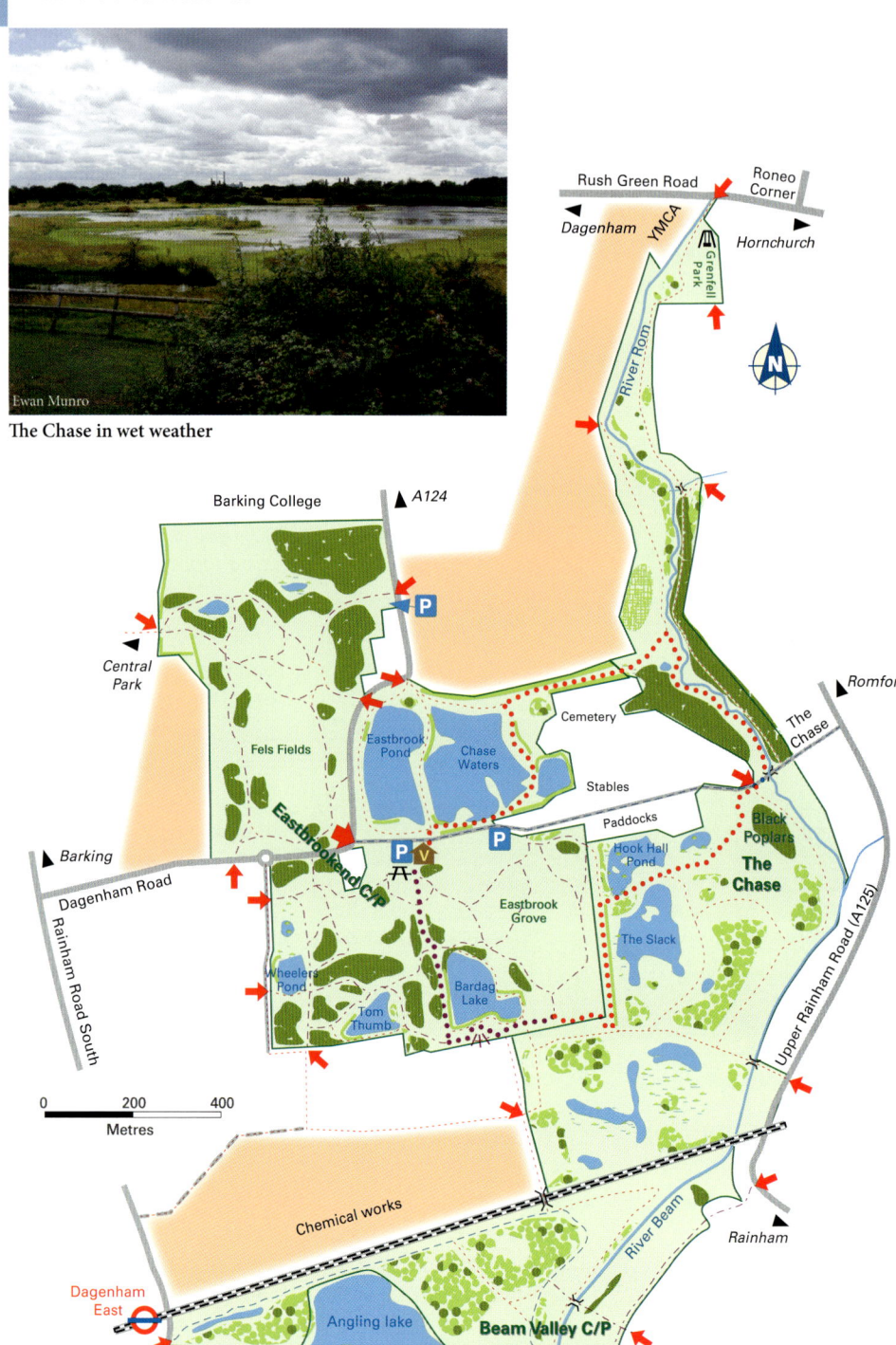

The Chase in wet weather
Ewan Munro

Rivers and wetlands

Beam Valley Country Park

The London Borough of **Barking & Dagenham**

183ac/74ha   RM10 9EH   TQ 512 850

This recently created country park runs alongside the River Beam, from the railway in the north down to New Road in the south, opposite the Ford plant. The area has been partly worked for gravel, leaving a patchwork of wet and dry grassland, tall herbs and scrub. At its southern end a new wetland has been created alongside the Wantz Stream, which also serves as a flood storage area when needed.

Along the river kingfishers are seen regularly, and reed warblers and reed buntings breed. Dense wetland vegetation grows beside it in places, especially along the Wantz Stream in the south. Snipe and water rail sometimes find refuge here in winter. A series of ponds have been created and these support great crested newts and other amphibians.

Accessible from Rainham Road South (A1112) or Ballards Road (B178), with on-street parking. Alternatively, park at Eastbrookend visitor centre (previous page) and follow footpaths south and over the railway footbridge.

District line tube to Dagenham East. Turn right outside the station and the entrance track is about 50m down on the left.

Accessible at all times.

Cranham Marsh

32ac/13ha *RM14 3AU* *TQ 567 856* *LNR*

Cranham Marsh is unusual in that it is not associated with a river. A seasonal stream runs through the middle, but it is kept wet mainly by ground water filtering out of a gravel terrace to the north. It includes damp grassland, sedge fen and ancient woodland.

The two small woods consist mainly of hazel coppice, with some huge old oak and ash trees, patches of wild cherry and a grove of alder. Dogwood, guelder rose and spindle grow around the fringes.

The marshy grassland is grazed by cattle and is bisected by old reed-filled drainage ditches. South Marsh has a large concentration of betony and, in the wetter patches, southern marsh orchids and ragged robin. It and East Marsh also have large patches of the rare yellow loosestrife.

Birdlife includes migrants such as blackcap, whitethroat and chiffchaff, and resident woodpeckers, jackdaws and tawny owl. Kestrel and sparrowhawk nest in the large trees regularly, and sometimes hobby.

In summer the reserve teems with insect life. Its many butterflies include ringlet, small copper and purple hairstreak.

Yellow loosestrife *fl. July–August*

On the fringe of Upminster, with access via Park Drive or The Chase, with footpaths leading on to the reserve. On-street parking.

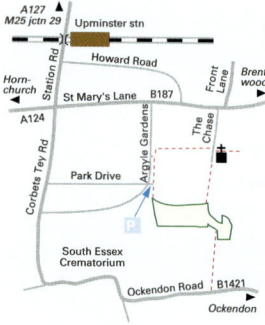

Upminster station is about 20 minutes walk via Howard Road and The Chase.

Accessible at all times.

April and May for early flowers and birdsong; July and August for wild flowers and insects.

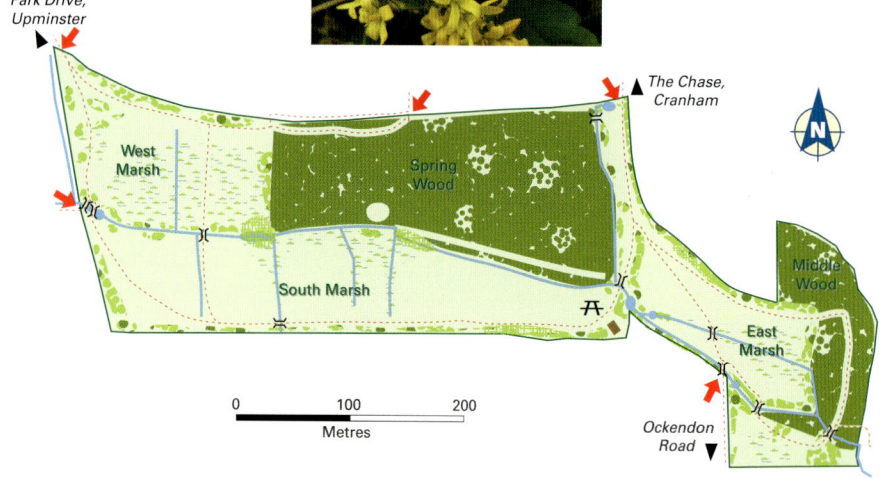

Ingrebourne Valley

This southern part of the Ingrebourne Valley, sandwiched between the built-up areas of Hornchuch and Rainham, has at its centre a prime wildlife site, the Ingrebourne Marshes SSSI, next to the former RAF Hornchurch, now Hornchurch Country Park, and surrounded by a number of areas of former landfill that have been restored. It is already a superb area for wildlife and can only get better as the restored sites mature..

Ingrebourne Valley LNR

371ac/150ha   RM12 6TS   TQ 535 848   SSSI (part), LNR

This Local Nature Reserve consists of Hornchurch Country Park and parts of the adjoining Ingrebourne Marshes SSSI, plus land adjoining the River Ingrebourne upstream.

Hornchurch Country Park was created in the early 1980s mainly on the site of an abandoned airfield, RAF Hornchurch. During World War II squadrons of Spitfires were based here that played a part in the Battle of Britain. Remnants of the airfield are still visible in the form of pillboxes and tett turrets.

For wildlife, the highlight is the Ingrebourne Marshes SSSI, a fine wetland next to the old airfield and further downstream alongside the River Ingrebourne. A wetland on this scale – with a huge reedbed alongside marsh and flood meadow – is very unusual anywhere, and especially so close to London.

Redshank, lapwing and yellow wagtail breed on this kind of wet tussocky grassland. Kingfishers make their nest holes in the steep banks of the river. Many sedge and reed warblers nest here, and also cetti's warblers, one of our few resident warbler species. Water rails can occasionally be seen prowling around in the tall vegetation.

Our smallest duck, the teal, overwinters on the ponds, snipe in the rough grassland, and bearded tits, and occasionally bittern, in the reedbeds. Barn owls can often be seen hunting over the open grassland and marsh harriers over the reedbeds.

With such a variety of wet and dry habitats the area is valuable for insects too. Banded demoiselles can be seen all the way down the river and it also supports several rarities, including the brown-banded carder bee.

The whole area is a stronghold for amphibians and reptiles, including marsh frogs that have arrived recently.

The visitor centre near the Squadrons Approach entrance, run by Essex Wildlife Trust, provides fine views across the marshes.

Ingrebourne Marshes SSSI

Rivers and wetlands

🧭 Main entrance off Suttons Lane, about 2km south of Hornchurch town centre.

🚌 About 1km walk down Suttons Lane from Hornchurch station (District line). Frequent bus services run from Rainham, Hornchurch and Romford.

🕐 Park accessible at all times; car parks open daylight hours only.

🔲 May–June for breeding birds; July–August for flying insects; migration periods and winter for birds sheltering in the marshes or plantations.

♿ Many surfaced paths suitable for wheelchairs.

🚲 Multi-use path runs all the way through the site.

Water rail *resident*

Cetti's warbler *resident*
Reg Mellis

Rivers and wetlands   137

Ingrebourne Valley Berwick Glades

22ac/9ha   RM13 9EJ   TQ 542 842   Forestry Commission

This is former farmland planted up by the Forestry Commission. To maintain the good views across the Ingrebourne Marshes towards Hornchurch and Elm Park, large open glades have been left between pockets of tree planting, and parts of this are carpeted with knapweed and other wild flowers. Skylarks nest in these glades and in the surrounding fields and flocks of fieldfares and redwings visit in winter.

Berwick Woods

50ac/20ha   RM13 9EJ   TQ 542 837   SSSI (part)

Berwick Woods is a former gravel extraction site that has been restored by the gravel company, Lafarge Tarmac. As well as newly planted woods and grassland, it has some established scrub and wet woodland around pits and ponds.

It borders Berwick Pond, used partly for angling but also part of the Ingrebourne Marshes SSSI and surrounded by large stands of reed, and it overlooks the flood meadows alongside the Ingrebourne.

With such a mix of habitats it attracts a wide range of our commoner birds and also some rarities – cetti's warblers and water rail can be seen – or more often heard, because both species are quite shy – around Berwick Ponds.

Access from Berwick Pond Road, which joins Hacton Lane, Hornchurch, to Warwick Lane, Rainham. Can also be reached from Hornchurch country park via the bridge across the Ingrebourne River.

Accessible at all times.

May for songbirds; high summer for butterflies and other insects.

Ingrebourne Hill

183ac/74ha   RM13 8ST   TQ 525 837   Forestry Commission

A former gravel extraction site that has been landfilled and landscaped. Its main feature is the hill that gives it its name and which hosts a mountain bike course.

The plateau at the top is rich in flowering plants and provides good views across the large reedbeds of the Ingrebourne Marshes SSSI. Bitterns occasionally winter there and marsh harriers are often seen flying across looking for prey.

Access from the south off Rainham Road (A125), north of Dovers Corner (junction with A1306); or from the north via Hornchurch country park.

Accessible at all times.

Summer for wild flowers and for butterflies and other insects.

Marsh harrier *resident*
Airwolfhound

Rivers and wetlands

Lee Valley Regional Park

*T*he Lee Valley Regional Park extends some 25 miles down the valley of the River Lee, from Ware in the north deep into London as far as the Thames in the south, straddling the borders of Hertfordshire and Essex. Apart from the wetlands described here, it has two large complexes of lakes in the River Lee Country Park (p.156) and Walthamstow Wetlands (p.159).

Cornmill Meadows

62ac/25ha   EN9 2ES   TL 380 012   SSSI

The Cornmill Meadows dragonfly sanctuary consists of wet meadows and pools between the Cornmill Stream and the Old River Lea. Unlike most of the Lee Valley waterways, both meander in natural channels. Consequently they have a much wider range of waterside plants including some scarce ones like flowering rush. Comfrey and purple loosestrife grow alongside the Old River Lee.

The area is rich in aquatic insect life, and especially dragonflies and damselflies – more than half of all Britain's species have been seen here. Banded demoiselles are among the most numerous and – later in the summer around the meadows – migrant hawkers. Among the rarer species are the hairy dragonfly and the white-legged damselfly.

Dragonflies are favourite prey for hobbies, which can sometimes be seen hunting for them overhead. Water voles nest in the river banks.

In winter large flocks of wigeon and teal gather on the ponds, often joined by lapwing and golden plover. Teal and waders occupy the shallow pools.

Leave the M25 at junction 26 and follow the signs to the Lee Valley Park. Park in Waltham Abbey Gardens or follow the B194 to the Cornmill Meadows car park.

🚌 10-minute walk from Waltham Cross station. Bus routes: 505 Chingford–Harlow or 66 Debden–Waltham Cross.

🕐 Accessible at all times.

📅 Summer for dragonflies; winter for birds.

Flowering rush *flowers July–August*

Hairy dragonfly *flies May–July*
Chris Gibson

Rivers and wetlands   139

Gunpowder Park

222ac/90ha   EN9 3GP   TQ 382 992

This country park opened in 2004, much of it created on reclaimed land previously used for testing munitions.

Much of the current wildlife interest lies in Sewardstone Marsh. This is wet woodland that regenerated naturally on pulverised fuel ash dumped into holes created by the extraction of sand and gravel. Over the years a tangle of dense woodland has formed, with a variety of willow species. In winter it attracts snipe, and flocks of wintering thrushes and large mixed tit flocks sometimes move through. With lots of dead wood and several shallow ponds it is good for invertebrates and amphibians also.

The Cattlegate Flood Relief Channel flows down the western boundary and to the north the Black Ditch, formerly used to transport goods into and out of the ordnance factory. These are densely vegetated and populated by water voles. Reed buntings, sedge warblers and reed warblers nest here.

Meadows have been created on the reclaimed land to the north, with areas of wild flowers and groups of trees, and 80 acres are arable farmland.

The main entrance is on Sewardstone Road (A112), south of the roundabout junction with the A121, south of Waltham Abbey..

The nearest train station is Enfield Lock, 15 minutes' walk away. Bus route 505 Chingford station–Harlow runs past the main entrance.

Accessible at all times.

Winter for birds; late spring through the summer for wetland wildlife.

The main pathways are wheelchair accessible.

National Cycle Loop runs through the site.

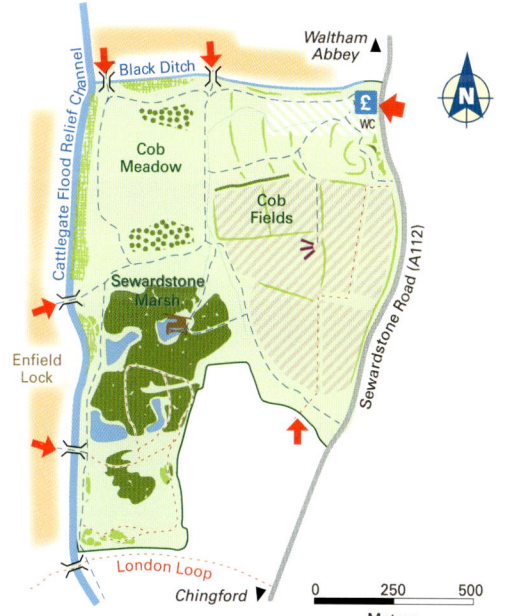

Sedge warbler *summer visitor*
Francesco Veronesi

Lee Valley Walthamstow Marsh

95ac/38ha   E10 7QL   TQ 354 871   SSSI

This is one of the last surviving marshlands in London. Formerly grazed as common land under the Lammas system (under which the grass was left uncut until late summer), it was being cut for hay until cattle were reintroduced in 2003.

This encourages wild flowers and over 160 species have been recorded here. One particular beneficiary of the grazing is creeping marshwort, a rare plant that likes the grazed edges of ditches.

Reed and sedge warblers nest in the reed beds, and snipe and stonechat visit in winter.

Belted galloways on Walthamstow Marsh
Gordon Joly

On Lea Bridge Road between Walthamstow and Hackney. Park (from 9.15am) at the WaterWorks Visitor Centre or the Lee Valley Ice Centre on Lea Bridge Road (A104) and follow footpaths from there.

Clapton station is about 10 minutes' walk from the Lee Valley Walk alongside the river, via Southwold Road. Regular bus services into London from Walthamstow and Leyton run along Lea Bridge Road.

WaterWorks open from 8am to 6.30pm summer, 4pm winter, others accessible at all times.

Summer for wild flowers, dragonflies and other insects.

Rivers and wetlands 141

Middlesex Filter Beds

10ac/4ha *E10 7QL* *TQ 359 865*

Built at the height of the cholera epidemic to purify London's drinking water, the Essex filter beds were closed in the 1970s. After that nature took over and created, in a relatively small area, a patchwork of different habitats, including open water, reedbed, scrub, wet woodland, and old brickwork that provides many crevices for toads, frogs, lizards and other animals. Reed buntings, coot and moorhen nest in the dense vegetation, and the area supports a wide range of dragonflies.

WaterWorks Nature Reserve

25ac/10ha *E10 7QL* *TQ 362 868*

These old filter beds have been renamed the WaterWorks Nature Reserve and are managed for wildlife. The visitor centre has interactive displays to interpret the history of the site and there is also a bird hide, built over the central well-head.

It supports a wide range of plants and hosts of amphibians and dragonflies. Birdlife includes little grebe, kingfisher and reed bunting, with teal and gadwall visiting in winter.

WaterWorks Nature Reserve
LVRPA

Rivers and wetlands

Mardyke Valley Davy Down

32ac/13ha   RM16 5UL   TQ 588 803

ESSEX & SUFFOLK WATER

THURROCK COUNCIL

Former farmland in the Mardyke valley that has been planted up and landscaped. It includes a pumping station built originally to house huge diesel pumps extracting water from a borehole in the chalk below, now replaced by an electric pump. It is overlooked by a 19th century railway viaduct.

It has meadows running along the Mar Dyke, maturing woodland, ponds and a small wetland. The Mar Dyke has water voles and has recently been colonised by marsh frogs.

Beyond the railway viaduct the Mardyke Way footpath runs through floodplain meadows.

On the B186 (Pilgrims Lane) between South Ockendon and Chafford Hundred. Leave the A13(T) or the M25 at their junction and head east on the A1306 towards Chafford Hundred/Grays, turning right where it crosses the B186. The entry is on the left about 200m up.

Bus services from Romford to Lakeside run along Pilgrims Lane.

Accessible at all times.

Mardyke Woods

62ac/25ha   RM15 5NG   TQ 585

Forestry Commission

A group of ancient woods on a hillside overlooking the Mardyke, originally part of the Belhus Park Estate and acquired by the Forestry Commission in 2002. The woods are quite diverse in terms of tree species and from the slope there are good views across the flood plain of the Mar Dyke.

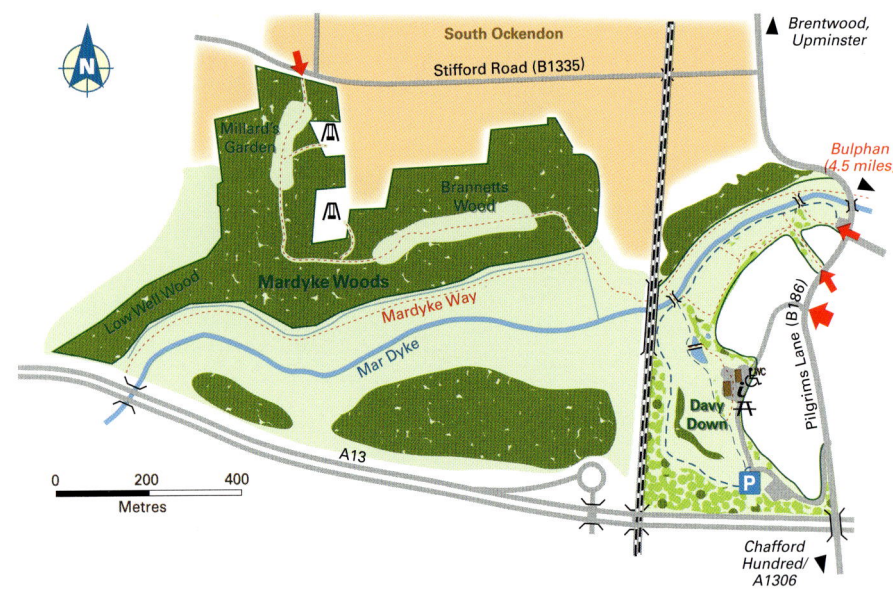

… Rivers and wetlands

Mayesbrook Park

The London Borough of Barking & Dagenham

99ac/40ha   RM8 2HG   TQ 463 844   LNR

Mayesbrook Park, on the border between Barking and Dagenham, claims to be Britain's first climate change park. It was a traditional urban park with the Mayes Brook running down its western border, but beginning in 2011 its southern section has been revamped as a 'demonstration of urban river restoration'.

Formerly in a sterile concrete channel, the Mayes Brook has been cleaned up and 're-wilded', and now runs in a natural, meandering channel within a specially created floodplain, so that it can overflow in wet weather without causing damage. Insects and wetland flowers have been quick to colonise the new wetland and already it looks as if it has been there for many years.

Meadow areas have been created, and trees and shrubs have been planted to filter airborne pollution and provide shade.

Alongside the usual mallards and canada geese, mute swans, coot and greylag geese occupy the two large lakes, and green woodpeckers and grey squirrels the wooded areas.

The restored Mayes Brook in Mayesbrook Park

Vehicle access from Lodge Avenue (A1153) in Dagenham, and also pedestrian access from residential streets to the west.

A few minutes' walk from Upney tube station (District Line): turn left outside the station and first right into The Drive. Buses run along Lodge Avenue.

 Accessible at all times.

Spring and summer for wild flowers and for flying insects around the lakes and wetland.

Rivers and wetlands

Roding Valley Park

213ac/86ha   **IG8 7JQ**   **TQ 412 902**

This recently created park follows the River Roding from Redbridge roundabout in the south to the borough boundary in the north, forming a Green Corridor through the west of Redbridge. It is a mixture of close-mown and rough grassland, sown with wild flowers, with small pockets of woodland and scrub. It has a network of surfaced paths.

Water voles occupy the river, and there is a good chance of seeing herons and the occasional kingfisher, flying low across the water. The river is an important migration route for birds, so during spring and autumn migration periods unusual species may turn up.

In summer the grassland and scrub supports many butterflies, including brimstone, gatekeeper and speckled wood. Dragonflies and damselflies along the river include broad-bodied chaser, common darter, banded demoiselle and white-legged damselfly.

For the Ray Park visitor centre, follow Chigwell Road (A113) from M11 junction 4 and turn left into Snakes Lane East. Can also be reached on foot from Roding Lane and Eastern Avenue.

Redbridge, South Woodford, Wanstead and Woodford tube stations are within easy reach. Several bus routes pass nearby.

Accessible at all times. Ray Park visitor centre open dawn to dusk.

Spring and summer for flowers, birds and insect life.

Cycle paths throughout, linking with through routes.

On warm evenings bats hunt for insects over the water. Wild flowers include purple loosestrife and, in the river, water crowfoot.

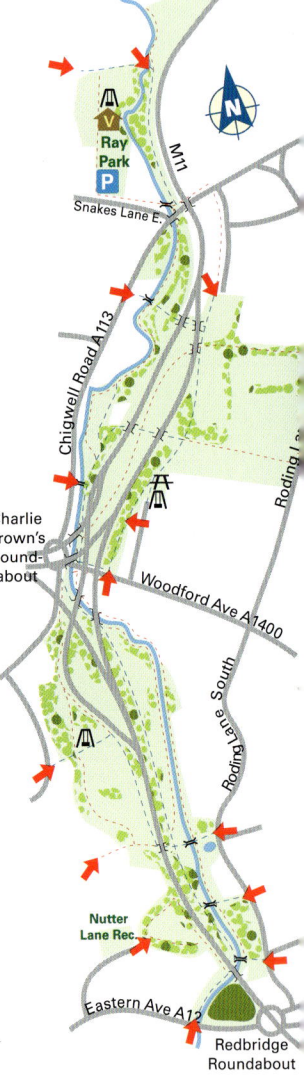

Tajinder Lachhar

Rivers and wetlands   145

Sawbridgeworth Marsh

22ac/9ha   CM21 9HR   TL 493 158   SSSI

This marshland nature reserve in the valley of the River Stort consists of an area of waterlogged marsh, normally under water for most of the year; a peaty meadow sloping up from the marsh to the eastern boundary; and a low-lying willow plantation to the south.

It contains plants which were once quite common but are now found on only a few sites in Essex, such as marsh willowherb and marsh valerian. Other uncommon plants include marsh arrow-grass, southern marsh orchid and blunt-flowered rush.

It has several open drainage ditches and two ponds rich in aquatic life. The areas of sedge, reeds and tall fen vegetation provide a valuable nesting habitat for reed and sedge warblers. Other breeding birds include snipe and water rail. In summer the marsh is alive with insects.

West of the road from Sawbridgeworth to Little Hallingbury. No car park, but there are two small lay-bys on the opposite side of the road about 200m north of the reserve entrance. Care should be taken since the road is narrow and traffic travels at high speeds.

About 800m north-east of Sawbridgeworth station: turn left outside the station then left into Hallingbury Road.

Accessible at all times.

Worth a visit at all times of the year but the spring and summer months are usually the most interesting.

Waterproof footwear usually necessary, even in summer.

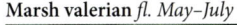

Marsh valerian fl. May–July
ceridwen

Stanford Warren

41ac/17ha **SS17 0RN** **TQ 687 812** **SSSI**

This is one of the largest reedbeds in Essex, created by gravel extraction in the 1920s, together with areas of marsh and rough grassland.

In spring and summer the reedbeds are full of birds fussing around, including reed buntings, reed warblers and sedge warblers, all of which breed. Water rail breed here too, but you need to work hard to see them because they are so shy.

Winter brings in bearded tits, grey wagtail and snipe – best seen along the Hassenbrooke, a small reed-lined river bisecting the reserve that crosses under the main footpath.

Another footpath turns off just beyond the footbridge and leads towards Thurrock Thameside Nature Park (p.165) through flower-rich grassland overlooking wetlands and Mucking Creek.

Reptiles frequent the rough grassland, and harvest mice nest among the reeds.

Access from London Road in Stanford-le-Hope. Turn south down Butts Lane then left into Mucking Wharf Road. Please park considerately by the former church at the start of the footpath.

About 20 minutes' walk from Stanford station. Turn right outside the station then right down Wharf Road. Access footpath on the right after the railway bridge.

Accessible at all times.

Late spring/summer for breeding birds and flowering plants; winter for visiting birds such as bearded tits.

Bearded tit *male, resident*
Smudge 9000

Reservoirs and Pits
Refuges for wild birds

Large freshwater lakes often form in former gravel pits, and many of our water supply reservoirs have been constructed where gravel has been taken out. The two biggest reservoirs in Essex, at Abberton and Hanningfield, are exceptions, in that they have been created by building dams across a watercourse.

Large lakes are valuable for birds, because they provide a safe place for breeding and, for migratory species, a safe refuge in winter.

Gravel pits sometimes have another advantage, in that removing the gravel has left behind free-draining terrain that is low in nutrients, and as a result becomes very rich in wild flowers and in the insects that depend on them.

River Lee Country Park in winter
LVRPA

Abberton Reservoir

1,240ac/496ha   *TL 963 185*   *SSSI, SPA*

Abberton Reservoir is of international importance as a safe haven for birds. Huge numbers spend autumn and winter there. The numbers of the top seven species – wigeon, teal, mallard, pochard, tufted duck, coot and black-headed gull – run into thousands. Added to this there can be hundreds of shoveler, gadwall, goldeneye, pintail and great crested grebe.

In spring there is the unusual sight of cormorants nesting in trees – this is common on the continent but rare in Britain.

Late summer brings the spectacle of large numbers of swans and ducks moulting – replacing their worn-out feathers – on the reservoir. Safety is vital while they do so because they replace all their flight feathers at once, which means that for a while they are unable to fly.

Since water levels in the reservoir were raised, creating shallow muddy margins, waders such as ringed plover, dunlin, ruff and black-tailed godwit are seen regularly on migration.

The surrounding farmland, too, is of value to birds. In winter thousands of golden plover may be seen there, along with small numbers of migratory geese and swans.

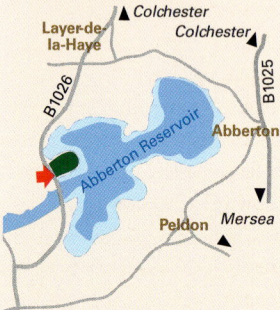

Five miles south-west of Colchester on the B1026, just outside Layer-de-la-Haye. Follow the brown signs.

Open daily 9am to 5pm (4pm in winter) except Xmas and Boxing Day). Collect a permit from the centre – free to Essex Wildlife Trust members.

Winter for wildfowl; May and June for breeding birds; August for moulting swans and ducks.

Wheelchair and electric buggy available from the centre.

Dogs allowed only in the car park and on the dog walk.

Wigeon *male*
Dick Daniels

Teal *female leading*

Abberton Reservoir Nature Reserve

59ac/24ha   CO2 0EU   TL 962 177

This nature reserve and visitor centre opened on higher ground in 2012 to replace the old ones lost as a result of Essex & Suffolk Water raising the levels of the reservoir. Areas have been planted up to develop into woodland and scrub, bordering a large area of grassland leading down towards the reservoir.

Two bird hides overlook the reservoir and rafts on which common terns nest, and a third hide overlooks the developing woodland. There are several ponds. Nature trails have been laid out giving access to all the habitats and to the hides. There are fine panoramic views across the reservoir and surrounding villages from the higher ground.

Brown hare, skylark, lapwing and various butterfly species were soon attracted to the rough grassland, which has green-winged and common spotted orchids, and dragonflies to the ponds.

Raptors including short-eared owl visit in winter and marsh harriers all year, and in summer common terns nest on the rafts moored nearby and grey herons in the heronry.

Good views of birds can also be had from the Layer Breton causeway south of the visitor centre, especially in winter when there is a fair chance of seeing smew, goosander or even bittern (and if it's really cold you can do the viewing from your car).

Common tern
Alan Williams

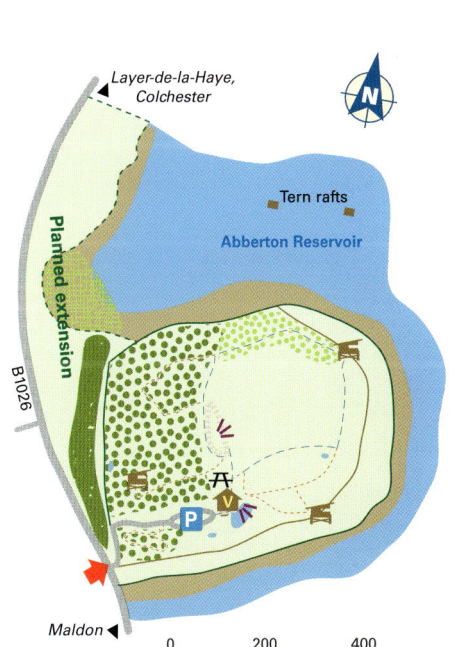

The visitor centre
Trevor Harris

Chafford Gorges Nature Park

163ac/66ha   RM16 6RW   TQ 597 795   SSSI (part)

ESSEX Wildlife Trust

Chafford Gorges Nature Park is in the centre of the Chafford Hundred housing development in Thurrock, near the Lakeside Shopping Centre. It consists of former chalk quarries now known as Warren Gorge, Lion Gorge and Grays Gorge, together with connecting land.

Much of it has chalky soil and as a result it has many plants that like these conditions and are unusual in Essex. The 'gorges' are surrounded by impressive chalk cliffs partly clothed with plants, and of great geological interest.

Grays Gorge

Formerly known as Grays Chalk Quarry, this is well known for its great range of wild flowers, including nine different species of orchid. Other unusual plants that grow here include common milkwort, fairy flax and autumn gentian.

A path runs around the top of the gorge and along here you can see pyramidal and man orchids in June. The meadow at the far (southern) end has adderstongue fern and is a good spot to see marbled white butterflies.

Lion Gorge

Large numbers of bats feed over the lake on warm summer nights. They roost in a tunnel leading to Warren Gorge – you can see the grille over the entrance in the cliff face at the southern end.

Accessed from the A1012 to Grays via Devonshire Road and Drake Road. The A1012 can be reached from the A13 east of M25 junction 30.

Nearest train stations are Grays and Chafford Hundred with regular bus services from both: nearest bus stop is opposite the medical centre on Drake Road.

Accessible at all times. Check the Essex Wildlife Trust website for centre opening times. The car park on Drake Road closes at 5 pm.

June or July for wild flowers including orchids; later in the summer for butterflies and dragonflies.

Dogs on leads in Lion Gorge please.

The lake in Grays Gorge
Glyn Baker

Warren Gorge

Much of the meadow in the base has been translocated from chalk meadows on land that has now been developed, and supports pyramidal and common spotted orchids, yellow rattle and kidney vetch.

In summer reed and cetti's warblers sing in the reeds, and kingfishers, hobbies or house martins feed around or above the lake. Birds such as pintail and pochard visit in winter.

Reservoirs and pits 151

Pyramidal orchid
flowers mid-June–August
Glyn Baker

Man orchid
flowers June–July
Adam Rochester

Common milkwort
flowers June–August
Adrian Knowles

Reservoirs and pits

Chigborough Lakes

46ac/18ha *CM9 4RB* *TL 877 086*

These are worked-out flooded gravel pits. The western section was left unrestored after extraction and as a result it has a great variety of habitats, including willow carr, open water, small ponds, marshy areas, grassland and thorn scrub.

Extraction has also left some low-nutrient areas with interesting flowers, such as common spotted orchids and wild strawberry.

Trees of note include a single wild service tree, a veteran oak pollard and two black poplar. It has eleven different types of willow, including almond and purple willow and several pollarded cricket-bat willows.

Breeding birds include great crested and little grebes, little egret, grey heron, kingfisher and increasing numbers of cetti's warbler. Smew visit in winter.

Most of the commoner butterflies and dragonflies can be seen in summer.

About a mile up the B1026 from Heybridge towards Tolleshunt d'Arcy, turn north into Chigborough Road. Continue past the fishery entrance and Chigborough Farm buildings, until you see the entrance gate to Chigborough Quarry. The reserve entrance is about 50m beyond this, on the left.

Buses from Colchester to Maldon Leisure Centre run along the B1026.

Accessible at all times.

April–July for birds, flowers and butterflies; October–February for wintering wildfowl.

Please keep dogs on leads when there is livestock on the reserve.

Easy-access path leads north from car park to a seat overlooking Gadwall Lake..

Smew *winter visitor*
Dick Daniels

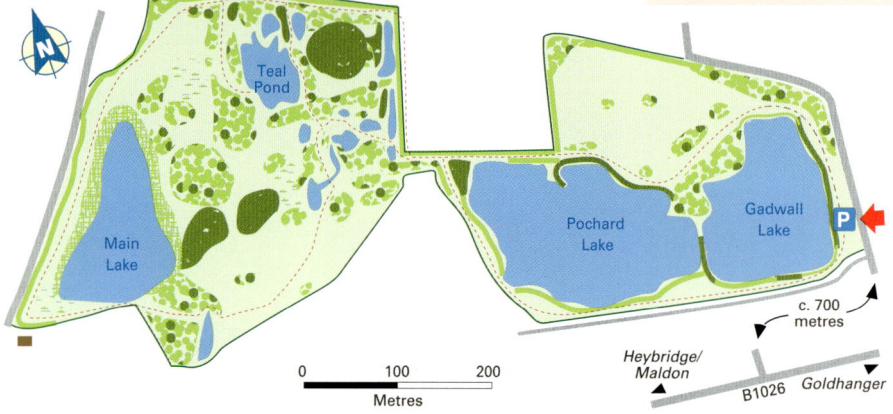

Great Holland Pits

40ac/16ha **CO13 0EU** **TM 204 190**

Gravel was worked here until about 1964 but the scars have virtually disappeared beneath vigorous growth. Habitats include heathy grassland, pasture, a remnant of old woodland, large and small pools, and wet depressions. From the high ground there are attractive views of Holland Brook meandering through water meadows.

It has a wide variety of flowering plants, including some that are unusual in Essex, such as moschatel, yellow archangel, small-flowered buttercup, mousetail, carline thistle and soft shield and hartstongue ferns.

Nightingales visit in summer and woodcock frequently use the reserve in winter. Resident aquatic species include kingfisher, coot and little grebe.

As you would expect of such a varied site, it supports many butterflies, moths and other invertebrates.

800m west of the Lion's Den pub at Great Holland, north of the Little Clacton Road.

Buses stop at the Lion's Den on the route from Clacton to Walton.

Accessible at all times, but car park only daylight hours.

Spring and summer.

Hartstongue fern

Reservoirs and pits

Hanningfield Reservoir

100ac/40ha   CM11 1WT   TQ 725 971   SSSI

This mixture of ancient and secondary woodland south of Hanningfield Reservoir is managed by Essex Wildlife Trust on lease from Essex & Suffolk Water.

The reservoir is best known (apart from its large trout!) for its populations of waterfowl. Gadwall, tufted duck and pochard are three of the important breeding species and year-round coot numbers are nationally important. Many geese, ducks and swans use the reservoir as a safe refuge in winter, and notably large flocks of wigeon.

An unusual summer spectacle is the sight of thousands of swifts, swallows and martins feeding over the water during peak fly hatches. Another is the bat rush hour around dusk, when hundreds of soprano pipistrelles roosting in the roof of the visitor centre come out to feed.

This section of the reservoir is surrounded by woodland. Well Wood and Hawks Wood are ancient in origin. Ditch-and-bank boundaries mark the extent of the old coppice, and some of the original hornbeam trees survive. The woods support many species indicative of ancient woodland and provide a fine show of spring flowers, in particular bluebells, yellow archangel and stitchwort. In summer, many dragonflies and damselflies can be seen around the ponds.

From the visitor centre waymarked trails lead through the woodland to four birdwatching hides. Much of the reservoir can be scanned from the hides, with especially good views over an island that is popular with wildfowl and a raft provided for terns to nest.

Broad-bodied chaser
female, flies mid-May–July

Coot *resident*

Gadwall *male, resident*
Alan Williams

Reservoirs and pits 155

Turn off the B1007 (Billericay–Chelmsford) on to Downham Road and turn left on to Hawkswood Road. The entrance is just beyond the causeway, opposite Crowsheath Lane.

Wickford–Chelmsford bus to Downham village and walk 800m down Crowsheath Lane.

Open daily 9am–5pm (4pm in winter) except Xmas Day and Boxing Day.

April–July for breeding birds in woodland and on water and for wild flowers; winter and migration periods for wildfowl.

Disabled parking and toilets at the centre; disabled pathway runs from there to a bird hide equipped for disabled users.

No dogs except guide dogs allowed on site.

View of the reservoir from the nature reserve
Glyn Baker

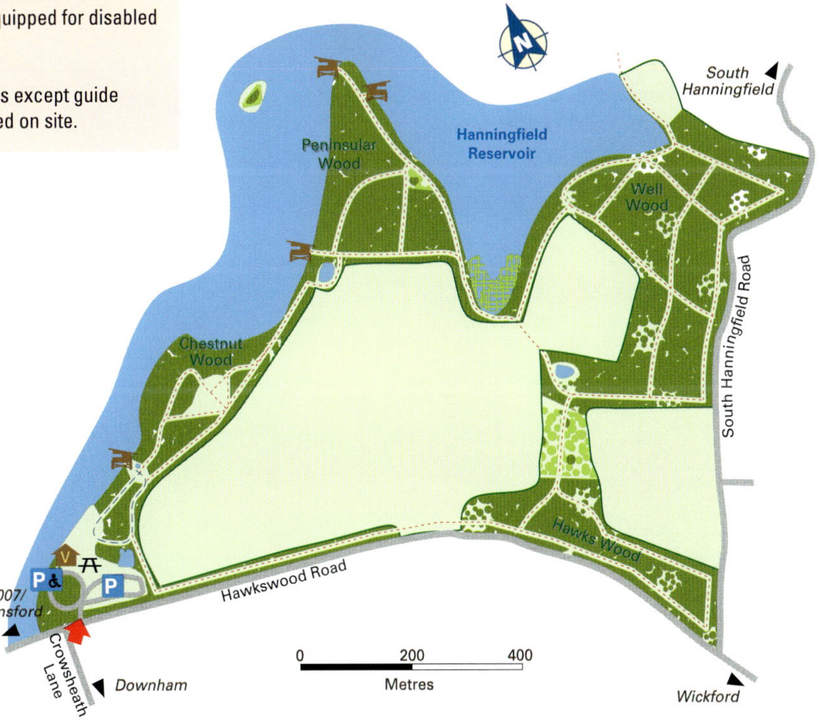

156 | Reservoirs and pits

River Lee Country Park

1000ac/405ha   EN9 1XQ   TL 377 033

The gravel beds of the Lee Valley were left behind by retreating ice at the end of the last Ice Age 10,000 years ago. There has been massive extraction since the 1920s and this has created a huge complex of lakes and marshes. The River Lee Country Park is at the northern end of the valley, north of Waltham Abbey and overlapping the border between Essex and Herts.

It's a tremendous – in every sense – place to visit, especially for birds.

For car parks on the Essex side leave the M25 at junction 26 and follow the signs to the Lee Valley Park. Car parks are also signposted from the B194 to Nazeing.

Train to Cheshunt station (Liverpool St line). Several bus services serve Waltham Abbey: routes 505 from Chingford to Harlow and 66 from Loughton are most useful for access from Essex.

Accessible at all times. Car parks open 8.30am to dusk.

Winter and migration periods for birds; late spring through the summer for wetland wildlife.

Many multi-use paths for pedestrians and cyclists: most also suitable for wheelchairs.

Bowyers Water
LVRPA

Holyfield Lake

Holyfield Lake is the largest of the gravel pits in the Lee Valley and has many wooded islands where birds breed and shelter while sailing is in progress. Goldeneye, goosander and smew visit in winter; yellow wagtail and sedge warbler join residents like great crested grebe and kingfisher in summer, when terns, swallows, martins and swifts often feed over the lake.

Cormorants roost on the wooded islands. The tangle of wet alder and willow woodland on the margins and islands also suits breeding warblers and nightingales. Grasshopper warblers, finches and green woodpeckers may be seen or heard in the marshy scrub and woodland in the centre of the island.

The path to Grand Weir Hide on the eastern side passes the Goosefield, where golden plovers, lapwing and canada geese may be seen in winter. Here there are several shallow pools which attract waders in summer and in migration periods.

The Oldest Pits

The lakes of Turnford and Cheshunt and North Metropolitan Pits are the oldest in the valley. With their varying depths of water and many spits and islands they have developed a varied wetland vegetation, showing all the stages between reedbed, carr and wet woodland.

Near Cheshunt Lock orchids (flowering May–July) grow on fly ash dumped from local power stations a couple of decades ago. A few hundred metres further north you come to wild flower meadows near Aqueduct Lock, where cowslips flower in spring.

Bowyers Water to the south has flag iris and expanses of water-lilies. Cormorants fish here and great crested grebes, mute swans and moorhens nest.

Reservoirs and pits

Seventy Acres Lake

New reedbeds were created here in 2002 and are now well established. The lake is a wintering site for gadwall, shoveler, coot and, most importantly, bittern, one of Britain's rarest birds – up to seven now winter here regularly.

Bittern at Fishers Green
LVRPA

Hall Marsh Scrape

This scrape (meaning an area of shallow water) was created on land backfilled with refuse after gravel extraction. Shallow pools had formed there and were attracting ducks and waders. Shallow water pools like this are scarce, so the pools were enlarged and sluice gates were installed to control the water level. Now redshank, little ringed plover and lapwing breed regularly, and teal, shoveler, wigeon and snipe visit in winter.

Hall Marsh scrape
LVRPA

Reservoirs and pits   159

Walthamstow Wetlands

521ac/211ha   N17 9NH   TQ 350 892   SSSI

London
Wildlife Trust

This nature reserve has been developed around some of Thames Water's supply reservoirs in the Lea Valley. They have been improved for wildlife such as by planting trees and aquatic vegetation; the 19th century Marine Engine House has been adapted to serve as a

Main entrance on Forest Road (A503). Limited parking on-site. Cycle/pedestrian entrances from Blackhorse Lane and Coppermill Lane.

10 minutes' walk from Tottenham Hale and Blackhorse Road stations (Victoria line tube and overground) and on bus routes 123 and 230.

Open 9.30am–5pm April to September, otherwise until 4pm.

Spring and early summer for breeding birds; late summer through the winter for wildfowl.

No dogs except assistance dogs allowed on site.

PLease respect other users of the site – it is an operational site for Thames Water and also a recreational fishery. Children under 16 must be accompanied by an adult.

Multi-use paths run through from north to south.

New plantings in the oldest reservoirs

visitor centre, and also has a swift tower; 13 miles of pathway have been laid out; and the Coppermill Tower to the south provides a high-level viewing platform.

Its birdlife is spectacular, and not just in London terms. Around 2,000 tufted duck gather in late summer, followed in winter by large numbers of pochard, gadwall and shoveler, and an occasional scaup. Having said that though, these birds are distributed across a large area of water, and sometimes you have to seek them out.

On the wooded islands there is a population of nesting cormorants and also a large heronry. Other breeding birds include kingfishers, little egrets, cetti's warblers, and both great crested and little grebes.

Peregrine falcons fly through now and again, and a variety of ducks, waders and songbirds stop off on migration.

The reservoirs just south of the visitor centre are the oldest and the most interesting for wildlife, with natural banks and mature marginal vegetation, that has been supplemented by new plantings.

The birdlife should get even better as these plantings mature, with the diving ducks that predominate now being joined by other species such as dabbling ducks that appreciate aquatic vegetation.

Shoveler *resident; male in front*
Dick Daniels

Tufted ducks *resident; female closest*

Great crested grebe *resident; chick behind*
David Harrison

Industrial relics
Nature bites back

Industrial relics, often referred to as brownfield sites, can develop great wildlife value, especially when they are what is sometimes described as *poorly restored*, in other words left to nature rather than tidied up and prettified. Canvey Wick is a prime example. Once grazing marsh, then a landfill site, then an almost-but-not-quite oil refinery, it is now one of the best sites for invertebrates in the area.

The normal thing for abandoned land to do is to fill up with scrub and trees. That will be useful to a range of mainly common species, but nothing special. The most valuable brownfield sites are those with a combination of poor, disturbed soils – that remain open and fill up with grass and flowers rather than scrub and trees – and a variety of unusual micro-habitats.

Abandoned railway lines also turn into attractive wildlife sites, given time and enough management to stop them filling completely with trees.

Finally there are landfill sites, best if hardly restored at all or restored carefully to make them valuable for wildlife.

Peter Harvey

Canvey Wick

230ac/93ha *SS8 0PS* *TQ 766 837*

Canvey Wick was once grazing marsh, then filled with river dredgings as the basis for an oil refinery that was never completed. Now it is Britain's first nature reserve specifically for insects. It supports more

Brown-banded carder bee

Peter Harvey

than 1,400 species, including national rarities such as the brown-banded carder bee.

Brownfield sites like this often have disturbed areas low in nutrients that are colonised by wild flowers and become ideal nesting and feeding areas for insects. Here, the combination of the original marshland, a variety of different materials from the dredging, plus the oil refinery infrastructure, has created a great diversity of habitats, from wet reedy patches through well-drained gravels to bare concrete.

Hence it has developed one of the richest populations of insects in the UK. The rarities are difficult to spot but marbled white butterflies are not, and there are lots of those about in July.

It also has spectacular displays of orchids and other wild flowers. These include introduced plants like goat's rue and everlasting sweet pea, alongside natives like birdsfoot trefoil and common centaury.

In the south-west corner of Canvey Island, between Northwick Road and Holehaven Creek. From Canvey Road (A130), turn right at two roundabouts on to Roscommon Way and then Northwick Road. The entrance is 200m down on the left.

About 2 miles' walk from Benfleet station via Ferry Road, Canvey Road, Roscommon Way and Northwick Road.

Reserve open daily from dawn to dusk; car park open from 9am – 5pm, or dusk if earlier.

Late spring through the summer for wild flowers (June for orchids) and for insects (July for marbled whites).

Some paths accessible for wheelchairs; kissing gates can be opened using a Radar key.

 Dogs allowed only on leads.

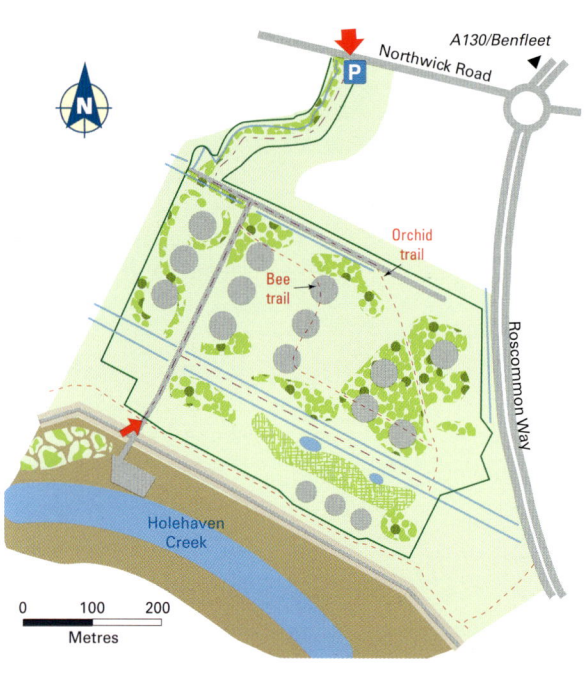

Industrial relics

Flitch Way

40ac/16ha   CM77 6RX   TL 519 212–TL 760 227

The Flitch Way country park follows the route of the old railway line from Bishop's Stortford to Braintree. The railway was built in the 19th century and dismantled in 1969. Since then nature has taken over, with the help of Essex County Council's rangers.

Sections of the line run on embankments with fine views over the surrounding countryside. Others run in secluded cuttings with banks that are rich in flowers, the longest of which is west of Dunmow. Near Dunmow conditions are very wet, and wetland plants such as water mint and hemp agrimony grow alongside the path.

The south-facing banks form a sun trap and are ideal for reptiles such as lizards, which can sometimes be seen basking in the open. They also attract many butterflies and other insects.

Can be entered at a number of points. Parking at Takeley (CM22 6QA), Rayne (CM77 6RX) or Braintree (CM7 3QL) stations.

Trains run to Braintree from Witham. Use hourly bus service Stansted Airport to Braintree via Takeley to return.

Accessible at all times. Centre at Rayne Station open daily 9am–5pm.

May–July for wild flowers, birds and butterflies.

National Cycle Route 16 runs all the way and is signposted through Gt Dunmow.

Hemp agrimony and water mint line the path near Great Dunmow

Industrial relics

Gunners Park

62ac/25ha   SS3 9QN   TQ 933 841   SAC, SSSI(part), LNR

ESSEX
Wildlife Trust

The original Gunners Park has been developed for housing and in compensation an area of land to its east has been restored as a nature reserve by Essex Wildlife Trust. Formerly this was used by the MoD to test artillery and consequently has been untouched by agriculture. Many of the original structures, including gun emplacements and batteries, are still there.

It is mainly grassland, divided by ditches and with patches of dense scrub and scattered trees, and a large lake with an island. This combination makes for good bird and insect life in summer. Goldfinches, linnets and whitethroats nest in the scrub and mute swans on the lake, and kestrels and barn owls hunt over the grassland. In winter, turnstones and sanderling feed along the beach. It is also a good place to see unusual passage migrants in autumn and spring.

The adjoining Shoebury Old Ranges SSSI is rich in unusual plants but its vegetation is very fragile, so there is no public access, but it can be viewed from Ness Road. It and its buffer zone are grazed heavily by rabbits, and the latter has a couple of badger setts.

Turnstones beside the seawall at Gunners Park

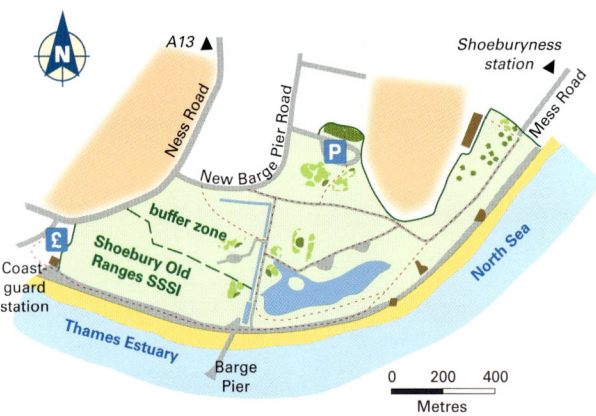

At the south-eastern corner of Shoeburyness. Vehicle entry from New Barge Pier Road, which turns off Ness Road (B1016) just before it becomes Shoebury Common Road. Turn off right at the yellow height barrier.

15 minutes walk from Shoeburyness rail station: turn right outside the station and, at the gates to the garrison area, continue straight on along Hospital Road. Turn left at its end then right on to Mess Road, which leads on to the reserve. Buses run from Southend centre.

Accessible at all times.

May to August for breeding birds and insects; autumn for passage migrants.

Industrial relics | 165

Thurrock Thameside Nature Park

120ac/49ha   SS17 0RN   TQ 693 805

What was once the largest landfill site in western Europe, at Mucking, is gradually being converted into a nature park. The first section was opened by David Attenborough in 2013 and further sections will open over the coming years as restoration continues.

It consists mainly of rough grassland and supports good numbers of skylarks, harvest mice and other small mammals, and also many reptiles. Its wild flowers attract pollinating insects such as bumblebees. Barn owls hunt over the rough grassland all year, and short-eared owls visit in winter.

From a bird hide and from the top of the visitor centre there are fine views across Mucking Flats and the Thames, where internationally important numbers of ringed plover and avocet, and nationally important numbers of grey plover, dunlin, godwit and redshank feed in winter.

Harvest mouse
David Corke

Accessed from Mucking Wharf Road, south of Stanford-le-Hope. Enter Stanford-le-Hope from the west via the A1013 and turn right on to Butts Lane. Mucking Wharf Road turns off left 400m down.

20 minutes' walk from Stanford-le-Hope station (Fenchurch St line). Turn right outside the station then right again into Wharf Road. After passing under the railway turn right on to the footpath across Stanford Warren nature reserve, which emerges on to Mucking Wharf Road. Turn left and follow the road to the reserve entrance.

9 am to 5 pm every day except Christmas Day.

Autumn and winter for migrating and over-wintering birds; spring and summer for wild flowers and songbirds.

An all-ability path leads to a bird hide overlooking the estuary.

Dogs allowed only on leads.

Wat Tyler country park

125ac/51ha   *SS16 4UH*   *TQ 739 867*   *SSSI*

This country park is named after the leader of the Peasants' Revolt of 1381, who lived locally, and like him has a chequered past. Originally part of the Pitsea Hall estate, it was grazed until the late 1800s, then taken over by the British Explosive Syndicate, and later the Nobel Explosive Company, to make and store ammunition. In the 1930s and 1940s it was used by the War Department to store materials, and after that for industry. It became a country park in the 1980s.

The past industrial use of the site has created some strikingly unusual habitats – nowhere else in Essex can you see mature woodland consisting almost entirely of hawthorn, for example, which normally grows under larger trees like oaks. The hawthorn hedges planted many years ago have spread to dominate the site, crowding other shrubs such as blackthorn, dogwood, elder and wild rose out to the margins. In places the hawthorn has formed a dense canopy under which very little else grows except for fungi in autumn. Elsewhere it forms impenetrable cover that is good for many songbirds.

There are many ponds, ditches and creeks both within and around the park and consequently in summer dragonflies are everywhere, including the scarce emerald damselfly.

The poor soil of the clearings and the broad rides is rich in wild flowers including blue fleabane, brookweed, yellowwort and vervain. On sunny days these open areas are crowded with grassland butterflies such as the skippers and common blue, and day-flying moths including the six-spot burnet.

Two hides overlook the saltmarsh and mudflats of Timbermans Creek. Wading birds and ducks often feed on the mudflats, especially when driven off the estuary by the rising tide. Further hides overlook Pitseahall Fleet, frequented by bearded tits, and the scrape on the landfill site beyond the fleet.

Former industrial buildings and some historic houses add further interest.

Hawthorn woodland at Wat Tyler

Industrial relics 167

From the roundabout in Pitsea where the A132 joins the A13 follow Pitsea Hall Lane south across the railway.

Train to Pitsea (Fenchurch St line), then walk 800m south down Wat Tyler Way.

9am to dusk all the year round. Café open daily 10am–3pm.

May–June for birdsong and early flowers; July for flying insects; migration periods and winter for visiting birds.

Easy access trail all round the site. Wheelchair access to hides.

Dogs allowed only on leads and not in the play areas or centres.

Burnet moths: *fly mid-June–early August*

Yellowwort *fl. June–Sept.*

Index of sites

	Ha	Postcode	Page
Abberton Reservoir	24	CO2 0EU	148
Abbotts Hall Farm	282	CO5 7RZ	102
Backwarden, The	12	CM3 4JH	38
Beam Valley CP	74	RM10 9EH	133
Bedfords Park	87	RM4 1QH	82
Belfairs Park	181	SS9 4LR	20
Belhus Chase	54	RM15 4XH	85
Belhus Woods	73	RM15 4XJ	84
Berwick Glades	9	RM13 9EJ	137
Berwick Woods	20	RM13 9EJ	137
Blake's Wood	41	CM3 4AU	13
Blue House Farm	245	CM3 6GU	104
Bowers Marsh	270	SS13 2EZ	106
Bradwell Shell Bank	102	CM0 7PW	108
Broaks Wood	62	CO9 1UP	14
Brookes Reserve	24	CM77 8BA	15
Canvey Wick	93	SS8 0PS	162
Cely Woods	57	RM13 9EW	85
Chafford Gorges NP	66	RM16 6RW	150
Chalkney Wood	81	CO6 2LD	16
Chase, The	49	RM7 0SS	131
Chigborough Lakes	19	CM9 4RB	152
Claybury Park	87	IG5 0XH	86
Colne LNR	34	CO7 9GW	111
Colne Point	264	CO16 8ET	110
Copperas Wood	14	CO12 5NE	33
Cornmill Meadows	25	EN9 2ES	138
Cranham Marsh	13	RM14 3AU	134
Cudmore Grove	42	CO5 8UE	112
Curtismill Green	48	RM4 1HP	37
Cymbeline Meadows	63	CO3 3LE	50

	Ha	Postcode	Page
Danbury Common	87	CM3 4JH	38
Danbury Ridge	106	CM3 4NZ	40
Davy Down	13	RM16 5UL	142
Eastbrookend CP	76	RM7 0SS	131
Epping Forest			
Around Chingford	300	E4 7QH	68
Heart of the Forest	900	IG10 4AF	66
Fingringhoe Wick	81	CO5 7DN	114
Flitch Way	16	CM77 6RX	163
Fordham Hall Estate	205	CO6 3LY	87
Galleywood Common	24	CM2 8JS	42
Gernon Bushes	31	CM16 7RN	64
Gilbert's Slade	51	E11 1PQ	72
Great Holland Pits	13	CO13 0EU	153
Gunners Park	25	SS3 9QN	164
Gunpowder Park	90	EN9 3GP	139
Hadleigh CP	121	SS7 2PP	116
Hainault Forest	118	IG7 5PG	74
Hainault Forest CP	100	IG7 4QW	75
Hanningfield Reservoir	33	CM11 1WT	154
Harlow Common	50	CM17 9ND	43
Harold Court Woods	27	RM3 0LA	58
Hatfield Forest	425	CM22 6LH	*76*
Havering CP	61	RM5 3PH	88
High Woods CP	134	CO4 5JR	89
Hillhouse Wood	13	CO6 3DU	22
Hilly Fields	16	CO3 3QJ	51
Hitchcock's Meadows	5	CM3 4FJ	39
Hockley Woods	109	SS5 4RQ	24
Hunsdon Mead	27	CM19 5EH	44
Hylands Park	234	CM2 8FS	91

Indexes 169

	Ha	Postcode	Page		Ha	Postcode	Page
Ingrebourne Hill	74	RM13 8ST	**137**	Stanford Warren	17	SS17 0RN	**146**
Ingrebourne Valley	150	RM12 6TS	**135**	Stour Wood	55	CO12 5ND	**32**
John Weston	4	CO14 8LE	**123**	Thames Chase FC	56	RM14 3NS	**78**
Langdon Hills CP	162	SS17 9NH	**48**	Thorndon CP	214	CM13 3RZ	**94**
Langdon NR	210	SS16 6EB	**45**	Thurrock Thameside NP	49	SS17 0RN	**165**
Latton Common	50	CM17 9ND	**43**	Tile Wood	6	SS7 2UN	**18**
Leyton Flats	75	E11 1PQ	**72**	Tiptree Heath	24	CO5 0PU	**55**
Little Haven	42	SS7 2LH	**18**	Tollesbury Wick	242	CM9 8RY	**124**
Lord's Bushes	53	IG9 5HH	**70**	Two Tree Island	259	SS9 2GB	**117**
Lower Forest	191	CM16 6TT	**64**	Tylers Common	28	RM14 1TS	**56**
Manor, The	70	RM3 9XR	**93**	Tylers Wood	12	CM13 3JA	**58**
Mardyke Woods	25	RM15 5NG	**142**	Wall Wood	11	CM22 7UG	**77**
Marks Hall Estate	182	CO6 1TG	**92**	Wallasea Island	110	SS4 2HD	**126**
Marsh Farm CP	142	CM3 5WP	**121**	Walthamstow Forest	51	IG8	**71**
Mayesbrook Park	40	RM8 2HG	**143**	Walthamstow Marsh	38	E10 7QL	**140**
Middlesex Filter Beds	4	E10 7QL	**141**	Walthamstow Wetlands	211	N17 9NH	**159**
Mill Meadows	36	CM12 9QQ	**52**	Wanstead Flats	182	E11 3QS	**73**
Naze, The	55	CO14 8LE	**122**	Wanstead Park	81	E11 2LT	**98**
Norsey Wood	67	CM11 1HA	**26**	Wat Tyler CP	51	SS16 4UH	**166**
Old Park, The	55	CM13 3RZ	**94**	Waterworks NR	10	E10 7QL	**141**
Pages Wood	74	RM14 1TQ	**58**	Weald Country Park	172	CM14 5QS	**96**
Parndon Woods & Common	52	CM19 4SF	**30**	Weeleyhall Wood	32	CO16 9AT	**34**
Pound Wood	22	SS7 2UR	**19**	West Canvey Marshes	257	SS8 0QA	**128**
Rainham Marshes	352	RM19 1SZ	**118**	West Wood (Daws Heath)	32	SS7 3YB	**18**
River Lee CP	405	EN9 1XQ	**156**	West Wood (Thaxted)	24	CB10 2SA	**29**
Roding Valley Meadows	67	IG7 6BQ	**53**	Woodham Fen	13	CM3 5XH	**120**
Roding Valley Park	86	IG8 7JQ	**144**	Woodside Green	26.7	CM22 7UG	**77**
Rowney Wood	83	CB10 2YA	**27**	Writtle Forest	100s	CM4 0RH	**79**
Sawbridgeworth Marsh	9	CM21 9HR	**145**				
Shadwell Wood	7	CB10 2HJ	**28**				
Shut Heath Wood	23	CM8 3ED	**31**				

Index of species photographs

adderstongue fern 44	dog's mercury. 76
avocet 117	early purple orchid. 32
banded demoiselle. 58	egyptian goose. 75
bearded tit. 146	fallow deer 12
bee orchid 144	fleabane. 58
betony 52	flowering rush. 138
birdsfoot trefoil. 68	four-spotted chaser. 107
bittern. 158	gadwall 154
black-tailed godwit 101	golden samphire. 110
blackcap 23	golden saxifrage. 14
blue-tailed damselfly. 98	goldfinch 90
bog bean 65	grass snake. 68
brambling. 94	grass vetchling 120
brent goose. 101	great crested grebe. 160
brimstone. 20	great spotted woodpecker. 23
broad-bodied chaser. 154	green hairstreak. 38
brooklime. 87	green woodpecker. 78
brown hare 104	green-winged orchid. 46
brown hawker. 98	grey partridge. 103
brown-banded carder bee. 162	grey plover 101
bugle. 44	grizzled skipper. 46
bullfinch. 56	hairy dragonfly 138
burnet moth. 167	harebell 98
butcher's broom 74	hartstongue fern. 16
cep 12	harvest mouse 165
cetti's warbler. 136	heath fritillary 11
chiffchaff. 23	heath spotted orchid 42
common blue damselfly 130	herb paris 15
common cow-wheat 24	kestrel 127
common milkwort. 151	kingfisher. 130
common spotted orchid 52	lapwing 107
common tern. 149	lily of the valley. 41
coot. 154	linnet. 56
corn bunting 103	little grebe 125
cuckoo flower. 52	little owl 97
death cap. 12	little ringed plover 131
devilsbit scabious 52	little tern. 2

Indexes   **171**

man orchid ...151	sea holly...113
mandarin duck ...65	sea kale ...113
marsh frog...119	sea lavender...103
marsh harrier ...137	sea pea ...113
marsh marigold...144	sedge warbler...139
marsh thistle...	short-eared owl ...127
marsh valerian ...145	shoveler...160
meadow pipit ...56	silver-washed fritillary ...11
merlin...127	skylark ...73
moschatel ...34	small-leaved lime...16
mute swan...72	smew ...152
nightingale...115	sneezewort ...82
nuthatch...23	snipe...131
otter ...130	snow bunting ...121
ox-eye daisy ...88	speckled wood...37
oxlip ...11	stag beetle...111
oystercatcher...108	sweet woodruff ...32
pepper saxifrage ...123	teal ...148
primrose...165	tormentil...71
purple emperor...11	treecreeper...23
purple hairstreak ...47	tufted duck ...160
purple loosestrife...54	turnstone...164
pyramidal orchid ...151	turtle dove...55
ragged robin ...27	twayblade ...13
red bartsia...31	water rail...136
red campion ...71	water violet...65
red deer...83	water vole...50
redshank ...128	white admiral ...11
reed bunting ...119	white-letter hairstreak ...22
reed warbler...106	whitethroat ...90
restharrow...125	wigeon...148
ringed plover...108	wild strawberry ...165
ringlet...165	yellow archangel ...33
ruddy darter ...130	yellow horned-poppy...113
sanicle ...28	yellow loosestrife...134
scarce emerald damselfly ...116	yellow rattle ...30
sea bindweed...113	yellow wort ...167